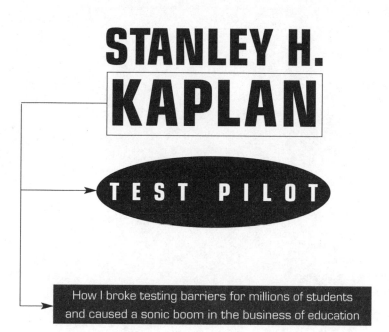

STANLEY H. KAPLAN

TEST PILOT

How I broke testing barriers for millions of students
and caused a sonic boom in the business of education

STANLEY H. KAPLAN
with Anne Farris

SIMON & SCHUSTER

NEW YORK　LONDON　TORONTO　SYDNEY　SINGAPORE

SIMON & SCHUSTER
Rockefeller Center
1230 Avenue of the Americas
New York, NY 10020

SIMON & SCHUSTER and colophon are registered trademarks
of Simon & Schuster, Inc.

Designed by Maura Fadden Rosenthal/mspaceny

Manufactured in the United States of America

10   9   8   7   6   5   4   3   2   1

Library of Congress Cataloging-in-Publication Data
Kaplan, Stanley H. (Stanley Henry), date.
    Stanley H. Kaplan, test pilot : how I broke testing barriers for millions of
students and caused a sonic boom in the business of education / Stanley H.
Kaplan with Anne Farris.
        p. cm
    1. Kaplan, Stanley H. (Stanley Henry), date.   2.   Kaplan
Educational Centers (Firm : New York, N.Y.)   3. Teachers—United
States—Biography.   4. Educational tests and measurements—
United States.   I. Farris, Anne.   II. Title.
LA2317.K27   A3 2001
378.1'662'092—dc21
    [B]   2001042628

ISBN 0-7432-0168-X

Acknowledgments

For the production of this book, I owe debts of gratitude to more people than I can possibly acknowledge.

I would like to thank my literary agent, Karen Ganz, and my editor at Simon & Schuster, Maureen McMahon, who possessed the vision to make this book a reality.

I would like to thank the core group of people who supported me in researching, writing, and editing the book. Anne Farris has been my invaluable collaborator. Anvernette Hanna provided her insights as an editor and researcher in the final phases. Fred Danzig, my former senior vice president who had been with Kaplan since 1972, contributed his seasoned eye to my story. And a big round of applause goes to Lynn McNutt, Doree Shafrir, and the rest of my office staff, who diligently persevered with patience and quick wit.

I wish to thank the former students and Kaplan employees, past and present, who helped recreate the pivotal events in this book. They include Robert Baraf, Ina Bendis, Ron Blumenthal, Deborah Bond-Upson, Michael Cirigliano, David Cleland, Dan Codianni, Jeff Cohen, Ruth Drucker, Charlotte Frank, Julian Frankenberg, David Gilfor, Chris Halem, Gloria Heiden, Tina Heiman, Catherine Huang, Rochelle Kaplan, John Keller, Peter Kneissl, Wendy Kopp, Bill Landberg, Cliff Lazzaro, Josh Levenson, Judy Levy, Aaron Peebles, David Philbrick, Bill and Judy Prest, Marilyn Rymniak, Lucille Sangiorgio, Nancy Strong, Ruth Sutton, Marc Trussel, Bob Verini, Carol Weinbaum, Barry Wexler, and Faith Wittner.

My thanks to the College Board, which went out of its way to meet my requests for factual and historical information in a timely and friendly manner.

And finally, double kudos to my family members—to my wife Rita, my children Susan, Nancy, and Paul, my brother Sidney and his wife Bea, my sister Rosalie and her husband Gene, and all my nephews and nieces. Over the years they recounted their experiences at Kaplan, which helped me write the rich history and feel the excitement of Kaplan once again.

*This book is dedicated to my family and to my students,
whose encouragement and input made Kaplan Test Preparation
a household name throughout the world.*

Contents

A BUSINESS GROWS IN BROOKLYN

People are often surprised to hear that, unlike General Mills' mythical Betty Crocker, there really is a Stanley H. Kaplan behind Kaplan, Inc. They always ask me, "How did you get started in the test preparation business?" The answer is simple. I started from the day I was born—or just about. I loved to teach—to plant new ideas—and that interest never waned. The saga of my success is a serendipitous combination of seized opportunity, perseverance, and a lifelong devotion to teaching.

My success is rooted in my Brooklyn childhood, when I was nurtured by my immigrant parents' values of tradition and education, and my mother's pleasure derived from her children's achievements. Never in my wildest dreams would I have predicted that my business of tutoring a few students in my parents' home sixty years ago would eventually swell into a vast international enterprise.

My story begins in 1921 in the New York neighborhood of Flatbush, where my parents, Julius and Ericka Kaplan, bought a house on Avenue K. I was two years old at the time; my brother, Sidney, was four; and my sister, Rosalie, was not yet born. Like other young couples, my parents moved to Brooklyn in search of open space and abundant affordable housing. There was a growing demand for my parents' plumbing and heating business. The roads were not yet paved, but the local public schools were top-notch, and that was important to first- and second-generation immigrant families who knew education was the key to success in America.

Our beige two-story stucco house had a small swath of grass in the front yard and a single pine tree in the backyard where the birds had established their own neighborhood of nests. This house was my parents' paradise and their stake in the unlimited opportunities of America. My father was a Jewish immigrant with only a sixth-grade education, but he appreciated the value of education and the rewards of hard work. He arrived in New York in 1894 from Slutsk, Byelorussia, with his widowed father, two brothers, and three sisters. Like many other Jewish, Irish, and German immigrants of that era, they settled on the Lower East Side of Manhattan in a tenement with no indoor plumbing. My grandfather sold fruit from a pushcart to support his children.

As a young man, my father devoted himself to building a successful plumbing and heating business. In 1915, his sister introduced him to a schoolmate named Ericka Herson, who immediately charmed him with her gusto and quick wit. Ericka had been born in Riga, Latvia, to well-educated and well-to-do German parents. Her grandfather had been the Chief Rabbi of the synagogue in Prague. They had moved to Latvia from Czechoslovakia to escape religious persecution. My father courted my mother on spring evenings in a horse and carriage he drove through the streets of Harlem. Although Ericka's parents spoke only German, my father spoke Yiddish and could converse well enough to make his intentions clear. They were married in 1916, and every year on their wedding anniversary, my father escorted my mother, dressed in all white, to dinner and the theater to celebrate.

My father was a quiet, gentle man with a burly, Babe Ruth physique. He was soft and round with no sharp edges. He loved to read and discuss politics. My mother was barely five feet tall, but her size belied her spunk and gregarious nature. She had the determination and ambition of a four-star general. Every evening after dinner, my parents retired to the front porch of our house to close out the day's accounting on their plumbing business. She kept the books, prepared estimates, wrote proposals for potential customers, and even offered advice on bathroom designs and fixtures. My father trusted her judgment completely and relied on her to make decisions for the business and the home. It was obvious that he worshiped her.

My mother, who never attended college, was determined that all of her children would. I'm sure when my brother, my sister, and I were born she swatted us on the backside and pronounced with conviction, "You're going to college." After graduating from high school, she took a business course and worked for a soda fountain manufacturer. Within a year, she rose to a top financial position in the company, and the owners treated her as part of the family. Such were the ties between employer and valued employee in those days. Like many women of her time, she resigned her job and worked in the home once she married.

My brother and I loved to read, and my mother made sure we owned plenty of books to line the walls of our basement playroom. Reading was like going to the movies because I could get lost for hours in the tales of fantasy and adventure. I read the Tom Swift series on inventions over and over again because I was intrigued by the innovations in the book, such as a telephone with a picture of the person talking. And this was the 1920s! For years, my mother paid a quarter a week to a traveling book salesman to buy the *Encyclopaedia Britannica* so we could find answers to our endless questions. Because we had so many books and my friends were always borrowing them, an idea struck me: Why not start a lending library and charge friends two cents a week per book? I made a little "office" in the playroom and launched my first entrepreneurial venture. I issued library cards, assiduously monitored checkouts and returns, and even charged late fees, although not very much—about a penny a week for each book. Some weeks I made a whole dollar.

My mother was a perfectionist whether she was keeping the company books or setting a dinner table. She was my best cheerleader, the reason I performed so well in school, and I constantly strove to please her. In fourth grade, I received a report card with all A's except for a B-plus in deportment (a fancy word for conduct). I stared at the grade on my card and couldn't fathom the thought of showing it to my mother—not because I would be punished, but because I couldn't bear to see the disappointment in her eyes. So instead of going home after school, I walked aimlessly around the neighborhood, trying to delay the inevitable. When I finally arrived home and showed my mother the report card, she questioned the B-plus. I told her I had been socializing in class. She said, "There's plenty of time to talk to your friends outside of class." And with that she dropped the matter. So much for parental pressure.

My mother's expectations of me were no greater than the demands she made on herself. When she was room mother of my kindergarten class, she produced a performance of a Mozart minuet, even outfitting me and my classmates in powdered wigs, velvet coats with tails, and long gowns. She played the piano while we danced on the auditorium stage. When the teachers needed something done, they called on my mom.

I also turned to my mother during times of trouble. One day while I was walking home from school, another student yelled at me from across the street, "Hey, you kike." It didn't sound friendly.

I ran home and asked my mother, "What's a kike?"

"It's bad word that's used by people who don't like Jews," she said.

"Why don't they like Jews?" I persisted.

"No reason except you go to a different church." I was only eight years old and felt confused and hurt. But she kept her explanation simple because she tried to get along with most people and avoid confrontation. In her own way, she was also telling me that I needed to resolve these confrontations myself, because she wouldn't always be there to protect me.

Another student approached me on the way home from school and pushed me. It may have been because I was Jewish or because he resented my straight A's when he was failing in school. Whatever the reason, I pushed him back and he gave me a bloody nose with a punch in the face. I ran home and my mother put a bandage on me and held me in her arms. But he never pushed me again.

One of my most vivid memories of my mother is her sitting straight-backed at the desk on our front porch, pecking at the keys of a Remington typewriter as she prepared tax forms and business contracts for plumbing jobs. Most small businesses submitted forms in longhand, but my mother wanted them to look professional and perfect, so she typed them all. That typewriter still sits proudly in my office. I lay on a daybed while she typed, and I heard the other children, including my brother, playing stickball in the street. I would join them later, but it was on the porch with my schoolwork and books that I felt most comfortable and confident. I learned early that I was more likely to excel in the classroom than on the basketball courts or baseball diamonds of Brooklyn. When my playmates chose teams, I was always the last to be picked. While my brother, Sidney, was a star at both sports and school, I majored exclusively in the three R's. My thrills came from academic home runs.

I advanced quickly through elementary school, skipping part of the second and third grades. Promoting the brightest students to higher grades was not uncommon in Brooklyn at this time because administrators were eager to ease overcrowding in the schools. One of my classes had forty-eight students sitting in six rows of eight. If we performed well, we were hurriedly sent on to the next grade.

My teachers were the personification of dedication, talent, and care. I'll never forget my fifth-grade teacher, Mrs. Holman, who rewarded our good behavior by quizzing us on math equations. I know that sounds crazy, but we loved the challenge. The class went wild with enthusiasm as we shouted out the answers. My fourth-grade teacher, Mr. Backus, told us scary ghost stories as a reward for good behavior. And he incorporated all the special effects. He would roll down the big green window shades and turn off the lights while our squeals of tantalized terror pierced the darkness.

Good teachers are born, not made, and I discovered my teaching niche at the age of nine. While other children played doctor, I played teacher. If friends complained about math fractions and percents, I would sit down with pencil and paper and explain to them how to solve the problems. Every once in a while, friends were reluctant to receive my help. So I would make an offer they couldn't refuse: "I'll pay you a dime if you'll just sit down and listen." With that persuasion, they eventually listened and learned.

I had a knack for zooming in on a student's weaknesses. There was no greater thrill than watching a student's face at that moment of revelation when he finally grasped an idea he had struggled to understand. Witnessing that was like hitting a home run and rounding the bases to the sound of a cheering crowd. His victory was my victory. And sharing in the achievements of my students ultimately became the primary reason for my success as a tutor.

My father's business was thriving, and we had a comfortable life. We took day trips to Coney Island in our latest-model Buick, and in the summer we drove to the Catskill Mountains for a week's vacation. On Sundays we went to the Bronx to sip ice cream sodas at my Uncle Harry's store, and I still have a photograph taken during one of our visits. Everyone looks so proper except my sister, whose mouth is agape and eyes are wide open. Who, other than she, would guess that she looked that way because I was giving her a good solid pinch on her arm.

I was infatuated with the latest inventions of our time. One day I read in the newspaper about an "auto radio" and wanted one badly. It featured the latest technology in portable radios because it fit under the dashboard and the tuning and volume dials were mounted on the steering column. I pestered my father to buy me one, and he finally consented to take me shopping one hot Friday afternoon in July. I still remember peeking out the window, waiting for him to take me to the store and wondering, "where is he?" When he finally arrived, we raced to the store, but it was closed. I'll never forget the disappointment of knowing I would have to wait until the store reopened on Monday. Those two days were like an eternity for a nine-year-old. When we finally bought the radio, my father compensated for the delay by driving me to Floyd Bennett Field. I sat next to him in the front seat so I could operate the new radio. Cool breezes swirled through the open windows while I played the radio really loud.

Other times we traveled to the country, where my father let me drive the Buick through open grassy fields. I was barely nine years old, and my feet barely reached the pedals. We zigzagged for miles, and I was king of the mountain. I loved cars because they were the shiny, newfangled mechanical devices that symbolized the dawning of technological development. Automatic ignitions with keys had replaced the hand-cranked starters on the car's front grille, and heavy rubber treads allowed for longer trips than the soft balloon tires. Cars also symbolized wealth and success, and I looked forward to the day when I would have my own car to show off. There were so many different kinds of cars, and I would impress the girls I walked home with by pointing out the makes: "Look, there's a 1927 DeSoto and a brand-new Studebaker."

I was ten years old when our comfortable lifestyle abruptly ended with the beginning of the Great Depression. It changed our lives and the lives of a nation. I remember the day it began. I was riding the bus to school when I saw a tremendous commotion of screaming people trying to get into a bank as the police restrained them. I was very upset by what I saw. When I asked my homeroom teacher what had happened, she answered with a somber and worried look. "The banks are closing, and thousands of people are losing their savings," she said. I worried about my mother and father and felt a pang of uncertainty and fear that soon became a reality.

My father's clients stopped paying their bills, his business nose-dived, and he sold all his stocks to pay his debts. He refused to declare bankruptcy and lost most of his savings. He became a broken man who never regained the confidence to rebuild his business. Instead, he took on small jobs and advertised with paper blotters that I delivered on Saturdays door-to-door in the neighborhood. I hated the chore because some homeowners angrily waved me away, but I learned not to become discouraged by the word "no." Sometimes the blotters produced a job for him, and that encouraged me to keep delivering them. To earn extra money for my family, I delivered prescriptions for a local pharmacy. The tips were my salary. I worked for a nickel an hour as a file clerk for my Uncle Peter's debt collection company in Manhattan.

I soon learned that the Depression was not a time for frivolous indulgences. One summer day when the temperature hit 100 degrees, I pleaded with my mother for a dime to swim with the other children at the neighborhood Farragut Pool. "No" was the nonnegotiable answer. "We can't afford such a luxury."

In 1930, I attended Seth Low Junior High School, where I skipped another grade. The stately, four-story white-brick school had been built only three years before, and a thousand students filled its classrooms to capacity. It was surrounded by three major thoroughfares, but behind it was a beautiful park where we ate our lunch and played softball. We came from a large area of Brooklyn, and most of us were from Jewish and Italian immigrant families. But there was a clear division in how deeply the hardships of the Depression penetrated. The wealthier students who lived in other parts of Brooklyn seemed almost insulated from the economic crisis. My family could no longer afford our live-in housekeeper, but some of my classmates' fathers were still buying fancy cars and fine clothes. I was intimidated by their sophistication and worldliness while my family was worrying about where the next dollar would come from.

But my determination was undaunted. I buried myself in schoolwork, and my teaching no longer was confined to helping friends after school. My German teacher, Frau Gelber, was impressed with my German diction (because my grandmother always spoke to me in German) and asked me to lead our class in reciting German phrases such as "Ich liebe dich," which means "I love you." The class shouted back in English, "We love you too."

And our principal, Isaac J. Bildersee, knew everyone's name and frequently gave us warm hugs, pats on the shoulder, or encouraging words to urge us on. His handwritten message on my report card read "We are proud of you, Stanley." Imagine a principal today signing report cards with personal messages!

Not all my teachers were exemplary. One particularly painful incident left me with memories of the kind of teacher I never wanted to become. Once a week, we gathered in the Seth Low auditorium to sing songs under the watchful eye of our music teacher. I was clowning around instead of singing, and my teacher reached out and slapped me hard several times across the mouth. Everyone fell silent in shock as my face turned white and I lowered my head in humiliation. I felt the stinging pain of disgrace and fought back tears.

When we were dismissed to the playground for lunch, a boy came to my side to comfort me. "She was wrong," he said. "Not all teachers are like that. You'll forget it." The boy was partly right. The teacher had been wrong and she wasn't like all teachers. But he was mistaken that I would forget. Children rarely forget the impact teachers have on many aspects of their academic and personal development. Teachers make powerful impressions on students' lives. Luckily, a good teacher can be just as memorable as a bad one. It was a hard lesson, but in this instance the bad teacher taught me how important it is to be a good teacher.

After two years at Seth Low, I entered James Madison High School in the fall of 1932. Like Seth Low, this school was brand new. There was an Olympic-sized swimming pool in a wing called the nautitorium. Over the entrance, carved in stone, was Madison's motto: "Education Is the True Foundation of Civil Liberty." The students were from Jewish, Irish, and Italian immigrant families, but they came from a much larger area of the borough, so I met lots of new people, including a group of very wealthy students whose fathers were physicians or executives at Macy's department store. I felt I wasn't in their league because I didn't possess the worldliness and confidence gained from playing golf at the country club and traveling to foreign countries. They lived a different lifestyle that both daunted and awed me. Once a friend took me with his family on a Hudson River boat cruise. We ate lunch in the ship's restaurant, and when the father left a seventy-five-cent tip, I was stunned. I had never seen such extravagance.

But I was no shrinking violet with my schoolmates when it came to teaching. My algebra class had forty students, and the teacher often asked me to lead the class while he sat in the corner of the room in a high chair with curved arms. I wasn't just playing teacher now, I *was* the teacher. And my friends would pass me in the hallway with the friendly greeting "Hi, Teach." One student, Aimee Rubin, was having difficulty passing algebra and risked being dropped from the National Honor Society. "Let me help you," I told her firmly. She caught on as if she were a math whiz. When she received a 95 on her exam, the teacher approached her and asked jokingly, "Aimee, did you cheat to get that mark?" She laughed and told him that I had helped her. I saw Aimee again at our fiftieth high school reunion, and she thanked me again for helping her. I also helped a fellow student named Marty Glickman, the school's star athlete, who later became an internationally renowned track runner and sportscaster. I helped Marty with some history homework, and he returned the favor by giving me tickets to a Madison High School football game. Our team won that game, nine to zero. Marty was short, but I can still see him running lickety-split over the goal line.

When I was a sophomore, Mrs. Leventhal, the school's employment counselor, called me to her office. I was a little nervous and thought, Why would she call me? As it turned out, her call set the course for my life. Mrs. Leventhal said she had heard that I tutored my friends, and she offered me a job at twenty-five cents an hour. I was overwhelmed. Twenty-five cents doesn't seem like much money now, but in the 1930s it would buy two tickets and a bag of popcorn at the local theater. Most important, I was being paid for something I loved to do. I was only fourteen years old, and I felt like a sandlot baseball player being recruited by a major-league team.

My first student was not as enthusiastic as I. It was a Thursday afternoon when I arrived at the home of Bob Linker, a bright eleven-year-old who had accomplished nothing in school but mischief. Bob opened the door, looked at me with shocked recognition, then made a quick retreat to the basement. His mother heard the commotion, and she and I chased Bobby down the stairs—only to find him wedged in a window frame as he attempted an escape. We tugged on his ankles to pull him back inside. He yelled, she scolded him, and we finally yanked him free.

Our first session finally began a half hour late at a table in the basement.

Bob was fuming with resentment, five chips on each shoulder, his eyes spelling out a challenge: "I dare you to teach me!" But I refused to be flustered or discouraged. I told jokes, asked if he played baseball, and tried to discover his interests. We talked as much about baseball as about math, spelling, and grammar. As I started probing, I discovered he liked math and was a fast learner. In school, he was a poor student because he didn't want to do anything that would please his parents. But I knew I had succeeded as a teacher when his mother called me two weeks later to say Bob wanted me to come an extra day each week.

I owe much to Bob. He helped me develop my teaching methods and discover why students have trouble learning. Most traditional classroom teachers at that time lacked a creative flair. Their teaching was rigid, strict, and boring to students like Bob. Information was presented without a lot of discussion or analysis by the students. The cycle of learning in most secondary schools at the time was memorize, regurgitate, forget. With Bob, as with all my subsequent students, the name of my game was to understand the student's point of view, present lessons in an engaging way, and offer encouragement. I told Bob, "I know this may be difficult for you, but you can do it."

Giving him small chunks of information to digest, I tackled the little problems first and then built on each accomplishment to reach the next level of learning. Most important, I showed him that learning could be fun. We played word and number games, and I used flash cards to organize and teach each lesson. One side of the card asked a question; the other side fully explained the correct answer. I never resorted to rote memorization. At the next lesson, I would quickly review the questions on the cards. Question and answer, question and answer—with full explanations. It had worked for Socrates' students, and now it would help Bob pass his exams. The question-and-answer method was used during the 1950s at the higher levels of education such as law school, but I discovered that it was effective, fun, and stimulating for students of all ages. Why wait to make learning fun? This method of posing questions that required students to learn through their answers would later become the basis of all the test preparation courses Kaplan offered.

Bob eventually won first prize in a national essay contest and attended a highly ranked university. He became a successful businessman, and fifty years to the day after our first tutoring session, he called me to say thank you. Success builds on success one step at a time—that was my motto.

I was becoming an academic extrovert and a workaholic. More than any other teacher, my eleventh-grade history teacher, Leo R. Ryan, stimulated my love of history and politics, and he coaxed me to enter a writing contest sponsored by the League of Nations Association. A month after submitting my essay, Mr. Ryan called me to his office, and I thought, "Uh oh. What did I do wrong?" When I appeared at the door of his office, he ran over to me, put his arm around my shoulder, and said, "You won first prize." I grabbed the phone on his desk and called my mother.

All during high school I was consumed by my schoolwork. My favorite book was *Return of the Native* because it conveyed the enduring lessons that good things happen to good people and the hero always wins. Believe it or not, one of my favorite subjects was Latin. It might have been a dead language to some, but it was real live stuff to me. In my senior year, I started a Latin-language magazine called *Vox Madisoni*, the "Voice of Madison." As a literary tome, it was rather limited because I'd had only two years of Latin instruction, but I wrote articles about current events, school news, and student birthdays. I even included jokes and riddles and a crossword puzzle—all in Latin, of course. I was proud of it because no one else thought of writing about the Brooklyn Dodgers in Latin.

When I graduated from high school, I was only sixteen years old, but I had ten paying students whom I tutored on a regular basis. My 1935 senior class yearbook contains a black-and-white photograph of me exuding all the moxie and confidence of a rising corporate executive. My thick jet-black hair was neatly parted on one side and slicked back to accentuate a small widow's peak. I was wearing a three-piece tailored suit—adorned with three gold scholarship pins—a stiffly starched collar, and a tightly knotted tie.

I had been accepted by Columbia University, but I couldn't afford the tuition. So I planned to attend the City College of New York, a free, public institution of excellent academic quality. I had been awarded a scholarship based on my scores on the New York State Regents Examinations, a series of exams on all high school subjects. But I almost missed getting that scholarship. When the list of scholarship winners was published in the *New York Times*, I scanned and searched for my name. But it was nowhere to be found. I knew I had scored well on the tests and my name should have been listed with the other students and near the top. I was understandably upset and called the Regents office in Albany to find out what happened. The Regents staff had made an egregious error and miscalculated my score. This was before the days of computerized grading, so there was only human oversight to blame. To its credit, the Regents board wrote me an effusive letter of apology and enclosed a computation of my test grades showing its mistakes.

So on I went to City College in 1935. I had more gumption and enthusiasm than most sixteen-year-old freshmen, but I soon discovered how difficult it was to rise and shine among a large group of older, more seasoned students. I didn't make many new friends at college and mainly socialized with friends my own age who were still in high school. I didn't have much time to make new friends anyway. When I wasn't studying, I was tutoring students. When I wasn't tutoring, I was studying hard and making great grades. My successes as both tutor and student gave me all the confidence I needed to keep pace with my older college peers.

I was making A's in all my courses until my sophomore year, when I received a C in biology—my favorite subject. I knew something was terribly wrong, so I immediately went to my professor. "Uh-oh," he said, "there's another Stanley Kaplan in the class. He received your A and you received his C. I'll change that immediately." Then I realized there must be a lot of other Stanley Kaplans. And there were. When I checked the phone book, I found no fewer than forty Stanley Kaplans, and, like me, some of them didn't have a middle initial. So to avoid relinquishing any more As, I adopted the middle name Henry. I'm not exactly sure why I chose Henry. It might have been my admiration for the novelist O. Henry, or it might have been those tasty Oh Henry! candy bars. But I've been Stanley H. Kaplan ever since. If someone asks, "What does the 'H.' stand for?" I immediately answer, "Higher scores, of course!" or "Preparation!"

By the time I reached my junior year in college, I had decided that I wanted to apply to medical school so I could earn a really good living as a physician. I had been earning more than just pocket change during my five years of tutoring, but I knew that being a physician would give me more financial security. I saw nothing but blue skies because my academic record was stellar: I was a Phi Beta Kappa, ranked number two in my class, and was the recipient of the college's Award for Excellence in Natural Sciences. I thought my only limitations to admission were geographic because I would need to attend a New York City medical school so I could continue tutoring to pay my tuition. My parents applied no pressure on me me to go to medical school, because it was expensive and they thought a tutoring career was best suited for me. What prescience! So at age eighteen—full of optimism, hope, and lots of A's in biology, physics, and chemistry—I applied to five medical schools in the New York City area and waited for the Fates to make the decision.

Then came a shocker. I missed five for five. I was rejected by all the schools. Failure was as foreign to me as a trip outside New York City, and the news came as a humbling defeat. Naturally I asked myself, "Why?" Talking to my friends soon revealed an answer. My Jewish friends at private colleges such as Columbia and Harvard had been accepted by medical schools. And my non-Jewish friends at City College were accepted at medical schools. Soon I made the connection: I was Jewish, and I attended a public college. I had a double whammy against me. First, an exceptionally large number of Jewish students were being accepted by medical schools and becoming doctors, and a concerted effort was under way to establish quotas on admissions of Jewish applicants. Second, because public colleges such as City College didn't appear to offer the same premium premedical studies as private universities, medical school admissions officials didn't perceive public colleges to be good breeding grounds for the best future physicians.

I was frustrated that I couldn't prove to the medical school admissions offices that City College students were academically on a par with private college graduates. The term "meritocracy"—or success based on merit rather than heritage, wealth, or social status—wasn't even coined yet, and the methods of selecting students based on talent, not privilege, were still evolving. There was no way to prove that there was a lot of intellectual gold in the public schools. There was no standardized test such as today's Medical College Admission Test (MCAT) to compare students from different colleges. In retrospect, I think about how different my life could have been if there had been an MCAT. I might eventually have become a physician with a thriving practice on Manhattan's Upper East Side instead of a leader in the test preparation industry.

Years later when my students complained about taking admissions tests, I told them about my experience applying to medical school. I encouraged them to take full advantage of the opportunity to show off their potential on a level playing field. Some people say standardized tests are stumbling blocks and barriers. But I remember the admissions process before standardized testing, and I believe tests open doors, not close them.

Did I cry a lot over the rejections? Absolutely not. I still had a flourishing tutoring business, and I turned to what I did best: teaching. I had a hundred students coming to my parents' house for tutoring that year, and I decided to focus on developing a business. But I had felt the effects of anti-Semitism and I worried that my Jewish name might hurt my prospects, so I changed the name of my business to Kaye Tutors. At first it seemed incidental. Jewish entertainers were changing their names, my students affectionately called me "Mr. K.," and Kaye was a nice American name. "Kaye Tutors—A Modern Educational Service," my brochure stated. "Individual Instruction for Those Who Seek a Greater Measure of School Success."

Yet almost overnight I realized I had made a mistake. I had rejected not only my identity but also my heritage. The name Kaplan originated from the word "chaplain" or "priest" and can be traced back to Moses' older brother, the first high priest of the Hebrew nation. If the name had been good enough for my ancestors for thousands of years, who was I to change it? So I switched back to Kaplan.

I proudly hung a shingle in front of my mother's house reading "Stanley H. Kaplan Educational Center." It was not a sophisticated operation. I had one business associate—my mother—and we ran a "mom-and-son" organization. She was my enrollment counselor, bookkeeper, secretary, and business confidante. Why didn't I teach in a school system? For two reasons. First, I didn't want to be part of the bureaucracy of a school system and I knew the joy of working one-on-one with students. Second, I wanted to use my own methods to develop my own programs. To this day, people still find it hard to believe I was never a teacher in a school system.

Not long after the Stanley H. Kaplan Educational Center was born, world events began taking control of our lives. The German invasion of

Poland in 1939 was the beginning of modern blitzkrieg warfare, and by 1940 America was preparing to intervene. Like millions of other Americans, I volunteered to join the war effort, but I was turned down because I was subject to severe asthma attacks. I felt out of place being left behind, but I seized the opportunity to build up my new business and help with the war efforts from home.

Parents from all over the neighborhood brought their children to me for help with the three R's. I sold war bonds to the parents, and I prepared about forty young men to take military placement exams for officer training school.

But the bulk of my tutoring business was helping students prepare for the New York State Regents Exams. The Regents had been administered in New York since the Civil War and tested students with a series of essay, multiple-choice, and completion questions. The Regents provided a minimum, uniform standard for teachers and schools throughout New York State. By the 1930s, scoring well on the Regents was the surest ticket for middle-class, public school kids to go to college—even private colleges. Immigrants in New York, eager to gain the advantages denied them in the old country, wanted their children to excel on these exams. So they eagerly sought me out.

Tutoring students for the Regents Exams, which covered a breadth of information, gave me an opportunity to use the Socratic question-and-answer method, which I found much more stimulating than a droning lecture. If Part I of the test had fifty questions, then, I would have fifty topics to teach. I was teaching what today is called "standards-based education"— teaching the basic concepts needed to reach certain academic standards. In this case, the standard was success on the Regents Exam. In the process, the students learned the concepts included in those fifty questions.

To help students prepare, I used a series of Regents study guides published by Manuel H. Barron, the founder of Barron's Publishing. Mr. Barron and his wife, Gloria, owned a college book store across the street from Brooklyn College and printed Regents answer guides on the second floor above the store. I was a regular customer of Mr. Barron's store, and I noticed that the Regents guides had some factual errors, so I dropped in at the store to see him.

"Stanley, I'll tell you what," Mr. Barron said to me. "Would you be interested in working on some of these books yourself?" So I accepted his offer and in 1943 began writing and editing many of his Regents answer guides. Over the years, I wrote sixteen different Regents study guides in the sciences, languages, social studies, and math. It was a great way to promote my tutoring business and give me exposure in the education and publishing world.

In addition to using flash cards, Regents guides, and encouragement as teaching tools, I had another secret that no one else used in the 1940s. It was a new piece of audiotape recording equipment called a Sound Mirror—a good name because it mirrored sound. The recorder had been seized from the Germans during World War II, and I bought a newly developed version of the magnetic recording machine even before the first tape-recorded radio show premiered in America on the Bing Crosby program. The Sound Mirror was a large, bulky reel-to-reel recorder with a handheld microphone and clunky clutches and levers. The tape was made of paper that was so fragile that I often mended tears with Scotch tape. It sounds antiquated now, but at the time it was the latest technology in magnetic recording and the first in a line of innovative machines I incorporated into my teaching program.

The first student to whom I introduced the Sound Mirror was Larry. He had problems remembering our algebra lessons from one week to the next, so at one session I told him, "I'm going to record today's lesson. Come an hour early next week and listen to it." It worked like a charm. After listening to the tape, he remembered and understood almost everything we had covered in the previous lesson. The recorder was a toy for him at first, but it then became a powerful learning tool, and he and his mother were quite happy with his high score on the Intermediate Algebra Regents. As a bonus I gave him a microphone to record his own sing-along tapes.

This was the beginning of a long-term relationship with the tape recorder, and I encouraged other students to review their lessons before and after our sessions to reinforce concepts. It was as if students were getting two lessons for the price of one.

The Sound Mirror wore out in two years, but I was now a bona fide technophile. I retired the Sound Mirror and bought Sonys. Eventually the technology evolved to cassette tape recorders—the answer to a Kaplan dream because they were small and almost indestructible.

Although I was developing new teaching methods, I never designed a grand plan for expanding my tutoring business. I always thought of myself as a teacher first and a businessman second because my motivation was to help students, not to become a huge financial success. But my catch-as-catch-can method of earning extra money was evolving into a solid business as word about my preparing students for the Regent exams spread around Brooklyn like a chain letter. I liked what I saw, and luckily, I had just enough business sense to seize new challenges and opportunities that were coming my way.

MY 54-YEAR LOVE AFFAIR WITH THE SAT

I'll never forget my introduction to the SAT. It was 1946. I was at the home of a high school junior named Elizabeth, who lived near Coney Island, to help her with intermediate algebra. As we sat down at her kitchen table, she said, "Mr. Kaplan, I need to take an important test. It's called the SAT. Can you help me?"

I had heard of the SAT, then the acronym for Scholastic Aptitude Test, but I had never prepared anyone to take it. The test had been administered since 1926 by the College Entrance Examination Board, a nonprofit organization of member colleges founded at Columbia University in New York City. These member colleges, primarily highly selective schools such as Yale and Princeton, had used the SAT for years as part of their admissions process. Now after World War II, more colleges than ever were using the SAT for admission as increasing numbers of returning veterans wanted to attend college with federally funded tuition. Harvard also used the SAT to award scholarships to needy students based on their intellectual capabilities, not their pedigree or social status.

Elizabeth handed me a booklet published by the College Board that contained a dozen pages of general information about the test, including a description of the test, fees, and test dates. It also included sample questions. These had been added to reduce the element of surprise for the students even though some College Board members had objected to adding the sample questions because they might promote "cramming" at the last minute.

I looked at the sample questions, and a broad smile stretched across my face. It was love at first sight. These questions were different from those on the Regents or other tests for which I had prepared students. For instance, one question asked, "Approximately 820 tons of water per second fall over each of the 11 gates of the Grand Coulee Dam. If the same total amount of water were to fall over only 5 gates, how many tons per second would fall over each gate?" I could see that the questions were designed to test students' knowledge and application of basic concepts, not their ability to regurgitate memorized facts. There were no pat answers. A student could take this test with an open textbook and still not answer the questions easily or correctly.

As I scanned the information booklet, my eye glanced at a statement that said "cramming or last-minute reviewing" had no purpose and was not advised. I remember thinking, "Not review for a test?" Now I was really interested. I wondered why the College Board would include such a statement.

"Sure, I can help you," I told her enthusiastically. This test was right up my alley, because it was an innovative test based on problem solving, not rote memorization. That was exactly how I liked to teach. I took the booklet home with me, wondering how I could help Elizabeth study for a test I had never seen. I spent the evening and next morning looking over the booklet and creating simulated questions. They were all the same as in the sample booklet, but entirely different because I made up questions on identical topics with new examples. The challenge was exhilarating. I was thrilled with the idea of teaching Elizabeth to think out her answers. Tutoring for the Regents was fun, and students learned a lot. But tutoring for the SAT would be more fun, because Elizabeth would have to think harder and apply a broader range of math and verbal skills.

In 1946, the SAT was a two-and-a-half-hour multiple-choice exam given nationally four times a year on designated Saturday and Wednesday mornings. Students didn't pass or fail but were ranked by scores ranging from 200 to 800 points for each of the math and verbal portions. The scores of each portion were added together so that the lowest possible SAT score was 400 and the highest was 1600. But in 1946, students never learned their test scores. They were sent to the colleges to which students applied and, on special request, to the students' schools with the condition that the scores be withheld from parents and students. A student had no idea of his standing in the application process when a college used SAT scores as part of its admissions consideration. The SAT didn't have the same influence in the admissions process in 1946 as today because the test was still not widely used, but more colleges were beginning to consider using the test scores in the admissions process.

The College Board was promoting the SAT to students, parents, and teachers as a well-honed research product designed to measure students' academic abilities regardless of where in the nation they attended high school. That made the SAT attractive to admissions officials because the quality of schools and grading systems varied so greatly from region to region. Some schools handed out A's like party favors, while others were as stingy with A's as Scrooge on Christmas Eve. And an A from a private school in New York might carry a different weight from an A from a Topeka public school. A student's grade point average (GPA) was a good indicator of a student's academic ability, but the SAT was becoming the nation's new academic yardstick. It could predict how well a student would perform during the first six months of college, and it could safeguard against grade inflation and poor, less demanding curricula.

I could tell from the sample questions that this systematic and demanding test would require a methodical approach to preparation. The SAT required a variety of skills, ranging from familiarity with the multiple-choice format to knowledge on a variety of subjects. I could see that some students would need to learn the information on the SAT for the first time, while others would need to review subjects they had learned years earlier. Elizabeth, for instance, hadn't worked with percentages or decimals since the sixth grade, but percentage questions were on the SAT math section. Few high school students would remember that $.2 \times .2 = .04$ and not $.4$. For her, I would be the Brush-Up Guy—no different from what I had been to other students.

The SAT also expected students to know not just the "what" of subjects, but also the more important "how and why." I remember the moment I learned this crucial difference in how we learn. My college science professor Dr. Goldforb was an expert in posing a question, finding an answer, and then reaching one step further. One day, he asked the class a question about a swallowtail's antennae, and I quickly raised my hand to volunteer the answer.

"Very good, Stanley," Dr. Goldforb said. But he didn't stop there. "But tell me why that is the answer."

"Why?" I pondered. "Hmm. Why." Reciting a factual answer was not good enough. *Why* was my answer correct? he asked. And *how* had I reached it? From then on, I encouraged my students to think things out, to think about the hows and whys. Learning to ask the hows and whys of information was essential in preparing for the SAT because it tested students on reading comprehension, problem solving, math concepts, and vocabulary skills with questions that required them to comprehend and understand the subject matter.

Teaching Elizabeth to prepare for the SAT was a challenge because it was different from tests students took at school. I could see from the SAT instruction booklet that there were tricky questions and even trickier answers with more than one good choice. Some of the choices were better than others, but there was only one best choice. Answering SAT questions required focus, reasoning, and practice. Acquiring test-taking skills is the same as learning to play the piano or ride a bicycle. It requires practice, practice, practice. Repetition breeds familiarity. Familiarity breeds confidence. Confidence breeds success. So I gave Elizabeth pages of vocabulary and reading comprehension drills, math problems, and vocabulary questions that I had created to simulate the SAT. I saw the results: she was becoming a powerful problem solver and a more confident test taker.

On test day, she had a clear advantage over the other students. She knew what to expect, and the SAT questions didn't throw her for a loop. She was able to tackle the questions using the strategies I had taught her and finished the test with time to spare. The test was, in her words, "a piece of cake," and she passed the word to her friends. When five of them called to ask for my help to prepare for the SAT, I suggested they all come as a group because I didn't have enough time to teach them individually and the tuition for each student would be much less expensive.

It was my first class to prepare students for the SAT, and it charted my path for the future. My first SAT preparation program consisted of four-hour weekly classes lasting sixteen weeks. The cost was $128, a charge that parents were happy to pay compared to what they would be paying for college tuition. "Go to Stanley Kaplan," students passed the word. "He can help you get into the college of your choice." A year after my first set of SAT classes, I had two hundred students enrolled for SAT preparation. Never could I have imagined the impending explosion in standardized testing that would leave me riding the crest of a swelling wave of educational change.

I began to think more about the SAT and how it affected education and students' aspirations. The SAT provided a more level playing field—and I liked that. It could help democratize American education by ushering a larger, more diverse group of students into the world of higher education. It could give students the opportunity to get into the top colleges without attending a prestigious private school or being the child of an alumnus or big contributor. A test like this one might have gained me entry to medical school, and I wanted one aspect of my tutoring business to be preparing students for a test that could help them get into college based on their academic merit.

Gauging academic competency has been the aim of admissions tests since their debut in America in the late 1800s. At first colleges used written essay exams to test the 4 percent of high school graduates who went on to college. But because each college had its own admissions test on specific subjects, it was difficult for students to apply to more than one college without studying for lots of different tests, and high school teachers complained that they couldn't prepare students for such an array of tests. In 1900, a group of twelve college presidents established the College Board, which represented member colleges and universities, to create order out of the chaotic system of testing and admitting students. Its remedy was to create a standard national entry exam that eventually evolved into the Board's most dramatic and enduring product: the SAT.

From its inception, the SAT was a target of criticism. Its creator, Carl B. Brigham, an associate professor of psychology at Princeton University and the Board's in-house psychometrician, had fervently endorsed scientific mental testing as a method to identify intellectual capacity. He issued the following disclaimers at the SAT unveiling: no measures can guarantee prediction, the test should be used as a supplement to other academic records, and placing too much emphasis on test scores is dangerous. Paradoxically, all his warnings ultimately became the same controversial points debated about standardized testing today.

The College Board said that the SAT, with its easy-to-grade format, met the two main criteria for an effective test: reliability and predictability. No matter how many times students took the SAT, their scores would remain about the same, and students' college performance was very close to what the SAT predicted.

The first SAT was administered in June 1926 to 8,040 high school students. It was a vastly different test from today's. The questions were grouped into subtests including word analogies and antonyms, number arrangements, logical inference, and paragraph reading. Here's a question from a copy of the original test: "Premise: None of the doors with latches are fastened. Conclusion: Some of the doors that are fastened have latches." Is the answer "Necessarily true," "Necessarily false," "Probably true," "Probably false," or "Undetermined"? Give up? The correct answer is "Necessarily false." That's enough to make one's head spin. But spin in a good way. It meant students were being forced to think and deduce.

It wasn't until the late 1940s, when America experienced an influx of soldiers returning from war, that the SAT gained a foothold in the admissions process. Added to this was a new group of students who, encouraged by their parents, realized that a college education could lead to greater success. Six times as many students took the exam in the late 1940s as in 1926. The pressures upon the College Board to meet this increasing demand finally prompted the College Board in 1947 to establish the Educational Testing Service (ETS), a private nonprofit organization near Princeton, New Jersey, to write, administer, score, and interpret the SAT.

My tutoring business grew exponentially with the increasing popularity of the SAT. In 1947, I earned enough money to buy my first car—a Super Buick—so I could drive to students' homes for individual tutoring rather than ride the bus or trolley. The Buick had three portholes and an automatic windshield washer I called a spritzer that was a great novelty to show off to my friends.

I was a teachaholic, but I also dated a lot, looking for Miss Right. I was ready to get married and settle down, but it just wasn't happening. So I struck a deal with my sister, Rosalie. She wanted to go to the University of Wisconsin, but my parents couldn't afford the tuition. So I agreed to pay her tuition with the proviso that she would find me *the* someone. For four years she delivered no prospects. Rosalie was looking for a woman who was ebullient, intelligent, attractive, thoughtful, a great conversationalist with a good sense of humor, and—because it takes two to tango—someone who would have me. Then at her graduation, in 1948, Rosalie called me and said, "There's a friend of mine from college I want you to meet."

Her name was Rita Gwirtzman. She had majored in social work and was a fellow Brooklynite. In fact, she lived only a mile away. On our first date, I invited her to the Lemonade Opera, an outdoor theater on the Brooklyn waterfront where free lemonade—my favorite drink—was served. I was immediately smitten by her. We made a great combination, because we could talk and listen to each other at the same time. She was a fireball; she talked a blue streak, but every word she uttered made sense. Her laughter charmed everyone. She was headstrong and believed passionately in social causes. And unbelievably, she enjoyed it when I took her on our second date to watch the construction of the Brooklyn Battery Tunnel and the three-level promenade leading to it. On our fifth date I popped the question, and she said yes before I could finish.

Her father, a successful accountant, was skeptical when I told him I wanted to marry his daughter. "A tutor?" he exclaimed. "My son had a tutor once. I paid him fifty cents an hour. How will you be able to support my daughter in the style to which she's accustomed?" That was easy to answer. I told him that my business was doing very well and my enrollments were growing by leaps and bounds. "You're an accountant," I said. "I'll show you my books."

Rita and I were married three months later on one of the few days I wasn't teaching. Of course, I took my faithful Sound Mirror to the hotel in Manhattan where we were married. I placed it behind the wedding platform, where my friend Joe squatted to monitor the recording volume.

"Do you, Rita, take Stanley to be your lawfully devoted husband?" the rabbi asked.

I whispered quickly to Joe, "Turn up the volume!" as Rita demurely answered, "Yes, sir, I do." My father-in-law became my accountant soon after.

○○○○

My days of driving the Super Buick to students' homes for private lessons were numbered. I began insisting that the students come to me, and soon the mountain was coming to Mohammed. But the apartment where Rita and I lived was then filled with students—students in the hallway, students in the bedroom, students at the dining room table. Our first daughter, Susan, was born in 1950, and Rita lined the bathtub with pillows to make available the only remaining play space for Susan. I knew then that it was time to move.

In 1951, we bought a two-story brick-and-stucco house on Bedford Avenue about a mile from my parents and one block from my alma mater, James Madison High School. The house was roomy, with two sun porches—front and back—a large dining room and living room, and a big basement. The house was perfect for a growing family and a school. And I had a new business associate in Rita. She was methodical, organized, and insightful—all the business skills I lacked to give focus and direction to my endless stream of ideas and ambitions. It was only natural that she would step in to help out, because we had daily demands right under our nose to keep the business books and tutor students. That's what happens when you run a business from your home. We all had big plans for the business. Rita and I gradually renovated the basement, converting it into classrooms lined with bookshelves. We installed a separate outdoor entrance for the seemingly endless stream of students.

They bubbled with excitement as the smiling bespectacled professor they had heard so much about took them to a never-never land of learning adventures. I gave the students name tags so that I could remember each one's name. Saying "Hi, Mary Beth" was much more meaningful and friendly than just saying "Hi." Encouraging and caring words could go a long way in reaching our mutual goals. The name tags were also useful in one class where one student was named Virginia Bruce and another was named Bruce Virginia. And the name Rhoda Ruder caused quite a laugh.

My challenge as a teacher was to give students the tools they needed to get the job done. I had to keep students interested, keep them learning, keep them laughing, and—above all—build their confidence that they could succeed. I was the gentle nudger. I wanted them to love learning as much as I loved teaching. I used everything imaginable to stimulate the students— arguing, joking, teasing, cajoling, listening, deciphering, and probing. I dug deep into my bag of tricks and pulled out mnemonic devices, monetary rewards, flash cards, scrawled blackboard diagrams, and flailing animated gestures. "If you get this question right, you'll win a dime," I'd tell students. Hands would shoot up in the air. Sometimes I'd give them a really difficult question. "This one is worth fifty cents," I'd tempt. Then pandemonium would break loose as they struggled to get the answer. But to earn fifty cents, a student needed to be able to explain the *how* and *why* behind the answer. Pocketing Kaplan coins became a symbol of pride and accomplishment for my students.

The classroom was my laboratory. If I listened carefully to a student's question, I could always detect the student's problem and tailor a solution. It was usually not a lack of ability but poor study habits, inadequate instruction, or a combination of the two that jeopardized students' performance. Not all students could grasp concepts with simple verbal explanations. Some needed visual associations. For instance, learning about geometric portions of a circle was easier if I drew a rectangular backyard and told my students to visualize the space a dog could cover if it was tied to a rope from a corner fence post. Suddenly intangible math concepts such as angles and radii came alive. Squishy math ideas took solid form.

My method, as it evolved, really was quite simple: Teach the students to be critical thinkers. My classes were not cram courses. Test-taking tricks and strategies would get the students only so far. They had to know the material, analyze the information, and think out the answer. I wasn't preparing them for only a Saturday-morning test; I was preparing them for a lifetime of critical thinking. It's like riding a bicycle: once you learn how to ride it, the skill is yours for life. And once you get the knack of taking a test like the SAT, it's also yours for life.

To learn a student's capabilities and deficiencies and to familiarize the student with the SAT, I created "quickie" tests or practice tests that simulated the real thing. I nicknamed these verisimilar tests based on the level of difficulty to tickle the students' fancy. When I opened a class with the Quickie Test NSAT, the students asked, "What's that?"

"This is an easy test. That's why I call it the Nursery School Admissions Test." Then came groans and premature sighs of relief—premature because it wasn't easy. A Quickie Test Eek evoked groans because it was rife with difficult questions. The name sounds awful, and the test was even worse. But I could tell from the quickie tests how a student would most likely perform on the SAT. My predictions were rarely wrong.

For instance, if students correctly answered ten out of fifteen questions on the NSAT, they would probably score the equivalent of 500 on the SAT. I also used the scores to separate students into classes. Sometimes, however, I relented in the face of passionate pleas from girlfriends and boyfriends who wanted to be assigned to the same class.

If I taught students a basic principle and they practiced applying that principle, they could answer most SAT questions. This was particularly true with basic vocabulary. "Memorize the word first," I told students, "then use it. See how it is used in different ways. You'll never forget it." I told students to go home and tell their parents, "I am impecunious. My allowance is paltry, and I need an augmentation." That left quite a few parents wide-eyed or scurrying to the dictionary.

I told students to think of all the words a young lady could use to call her boyfriend stubborn: obstinate, mulish, stiff-necked, pigheaded, bullheaded, contumacious, persistent, headstrong, obdurate, pertinacious, inexorable, intransigent, or intractable. "It's easier to memorize the meaning of those words because they have basically the same meaning," I told them, "and they all describe my wife." That prompted laughs. "If it helps to call me contumacious, fine. Whatever works."

Each week I instructed students to cut out ten newspaper articles and underline all challenging words. The more they read, the more powerful their vocabulary became. "Underline the words. If you don't know the meaning of a word, look it up in the dictionary," I told them. "Keep using the word. You can reinforce the meaning by seeing exactly how the word is used in the article. Use the word often enough, and it's yours."

I also taught them to use word roots, prefixes, and suffixes to help figure out the meanings of words. The prefix "eu," for instance, means "good" or "pleasant," such as the euphonious tone of a violin or a eulogy, meaning a positive speech about someone. "He was a bum all his life, but he was eulogized at his funeral," I told them. "So what does euphemism mean?" I asked the students. "I'll give you a hint. It has something to do with good." A euphemism is an expression describing something as being more pleasant than it really is. A garbage collector can be euphemistically described as a sanitary engineer. When a teacher catches a student with crib notes during a test and asks, "What are these?" the student can euphemistically describe them as "student reference cards."

Words can be fun, depending on how you use them. And understanding how to use words is one reason why reading is so important. I always encouraged my students to read anything they could get their hands on—magazines, newspapers, books, and advertisements. The more they read, the more they would want to read.

I encouraged my students to ask as many questions as needed. "You're allowed four hundred questions before I cut you off," I said jokingly. But seriously, I would have granted them four hundred–plus questions if needed. "Remember, there's only one kind of stupid question. That's the one you don't ask." Homework was essential. I developed pages of vocabulary lists, reading passages, practice tests, and math problems—à la the SAT—for students to work on outside class. "I am serving up success," I said. "Come and get it."

My SAT classes, although small, were sometimes loud and raucous when I threw out vocabulary words for a round-robin quiz. "She was a plucky girl to cross the street alone. What does 'plucky' mean? Look it up or you've made an egregious error," I told them. "Are screaming babies taciturn?" I asked the students. I hoped that from that day forward they would remember "taciturn" every time they heard a screaming baby.

The lessons worked. Here is a poem written to me by several students who attended one of my Sunday-morning SAT preparatory classes:

> Every time that he calls us contumacious
> We forgive him because he is so sagacious
> And even perspicacious, never fallacious
> His basic Quickies we shun as an aggregation of aggravation
> Due to this we sometimes hold back admiration
> Now last but not least after the SATs we'll have fun
> Having reached our zenith—and shown our perfection!

BEHIND EVERY WINNER IS A GOOD COACH

By 1950, three times more students were taking the SAT than a decade before, as more colleges used the test to review applicants. The College Board launched a public relations campaign to promote the SAT to college admissions officers, students, and parents as a shining new tool for uniform screening of academic performance. The College Board had a product to peddle, and it boasted in its handbooks that the SAT questions covered such a wide range of subjects that it measured a student's entire profile and not just selected features. Without the SAT, the College Board claimed, colleges would be completely overwhelmed by selecting their freshman classes from the large number of diverse students applying for college.

The handbook also stated that the SAT was misunderstood because unlike the old College Board essay-type examination, the SAT was resistant to cramming. From the Board's point of view, the name alone—Scholastic *Aptitude* Test—meant that the test was impervious to coaching because the College Board defined aptitude as "developed abilities" acquired over a lifetime of learning. Under that definition, aptitude could not be acquired through short-term coaching, the Board contended. The College Board told students and educators in its handbooks that coaching was unnecessary and produced insignificant results. The College Board made these coaching disclaimers to avoid accusations that students who paid for test preparation had an advantage over those who could not afford coaching. The Board also felt that coaching threatened the two most important features of the SAT: its reliability that students would score with consistancy no matter how many times they took the SAT, and its ability to predict a student's future performance. The validity of the SAT was at stake.

But I wasn't buying the argument. How could the College Board claim that coaching was ineffective? At that time, I couldn't prove that coaching helped raise students' SAT scores because the students didn't receive their scores. But I had firsthand knowledge that the SAT was coachable because I had witnessed score improvements every time students took my quickie tests, and I had student testimonials about improved test-taking skills. "Mr. Kaplan, the SAT was so familiar after taking so many of your practice tests," one student wrote. "I knew exactly what to expect. I wasn't so nervous. That allowed me to focus on my work, and I know I did well." Everyone performs better with practice. How could coaching not help? No one would enter a tennis tournament if he had never held a tennis racquet. I knew I needed to continually improve my materials and techniques to help students perform better on tests.

Although more students were seeking my help to prepare for the SAT, the mainstay of my business in the early 1950s was still private tutoring and preparation for the Regents Exams, and my basement was beginning to fill up like the Coney Island boardwalk on a hot July day. About a hundred students a week came for individual tutoring and classes to prepare for the SAT and Regents. How could I keep all of them on track? Once again I turned to technology, and this time I tape-recorded my class instruction—*live*. Students liked the idea because they knew if they missed a lesson or didn't understand it the first time, they could come to the basement at any time and listen to the class instruction tapes. Suddenly I was available to all of them at almost any time of day.

Then I thought, why stop with the classroom lessons? I could use the tapes to cover supplementary material and reinforce or expand lessons. I created what I called topical review tapes, each one focusing on a particular concept that might be on a test. If students were having difficulty understanding triangles, they could listen to a tape that gave them more information on triangles than they would need in a lifetime. I'd remind my students during class, "Don't worry. If you didn't understand fractions today, you can listen to the tape tomorrow. Or just come and listen to it again to reinforce the lesson." I also used the tapes with the quickie tests and called them "Test-N-Tapes." I hung big clocks in the classroom so students could time themselves while taking the test and then listen to a taped explanation of the test answers. This was particularly helpful if they answered a question incorrectly. For decades, these tapes gave my center a distinct advantage over other tutors, and eventually they evolved into an invaluable marketing tool.

Both Rita and I taught classes and managed the business in the early 1950s to accommodate the demand. But Rita also worked as a social worker, and I couldn't tend to administrative chores and teach at the same time. My school had to run efficiently, and I was never good at juggling management and teaching. So in 1953 I hired my first secretary, Peg Prest, and within a year I hired part-time employees, mostly housewives and mothers who were available during the day. I also hired smart college and high school students who could help write study materials, type, and tutor. This gave me time to do a lot more writing, teaching, and thinking. The most popular tutor was a bright college student who really set a classroom on fire with her animated lectures, rapid-fire questions, and witty explanations. She had been one of the best students in my SAT class, and I eventually hired her mother to work in the office. I was always on the lookout for friendly employees who were quick on their feet, were exceedingly bright, enjoyed working with intelligent, ambitious kids, and could handle a variety of chores. And if they were friends or family of current employees, all the better to add to the mix of our big "family business." Family and friends working together can sometimes cause friction, but most times it united the staff and made the office a warm and friendly place to work.

One key to my success was a dedicated staff. They shared my passion for the business, and we were one big, sometimes contentious, family. We lived the business and shared a sense of mission to help people change their lives and achieve important goals. Some of the people I hired for menial jobs such as dubbing tapes or stapling papers ultimately rose to top-level positions of responsibility in the organization.

Women didn't work outside the home as frequently as today, but I hired many women who wanted part-time work while their children were in school. They understood students' concerns and were always there to give them a bright, cheerful word. Peg Prest was a Wellesley College graduate who lived the business. Like me, she thrived on the energy of ambitious and motivated people. Sometimes I felt she was spending too much time tend-ing to the needs of a parent or a child, but then I realized there was never too much time for that. Every morning she bounded in the door with an infectious smile to greet students and prospective customers.

We had so much fun in that basement, which bustled with the activity of a three-ring circus. It was contained chaos—the single phone line rang constantly, parents were frequently dropping in to inquire about their children's progress, and students rushed up and down the basement stairs on their way to or from school or home.

The basement also became a place for making new friends. Teenage students came to study, but also to socialize and work off steam. I loved watching the intersection of lives and accomplishments. I remember a romance developed when an Erasmus High School cheerleader and a Lincoln High School football player met in a Kaplan class. I had wistful memories of my own days as a young man socializing and learning, and I was proud that my school was a bustling and energetic gathering place for young people. Over the years, there were many introductions that resulted in marriage. One couple wrote me years after meeting in my classroom that they were married and had named their son Stanley H. Murphy. Unfortunately, I never learned how Stanley H. fared on the SAT.

The basement had two small rooms separated by folding wooden doors where the staff tutored students privately while I taught Regents and SAT classes. I slipped into those semiquiet rooms to dictate drafts of the Regents guides and other publications. In 1954, Manny Barron asked me to edit an SAT preparation book authored by two Brooklyn high school teachers, Samuel C. Brownstein and Mitchel Weiner. The book, *Barron's How to Prepare for College Entrance Examinations*, was so successful that four years later we coauthored *You Can Win a Scholarship*. Like some other teachers, Brownstein and Weiner taught SAT classes in their spare time, but I was the only tutor in Brooklyn to prepare students for the SAT on a full-time basis. I was available to students any time of day and my classes were small and efficient with sixteen students, while Brownstein and Weiner had two hundred students in a class on the weekends. I thus had a competitive advantage over schoolteachers who tutored part-time.

Most nights it was 9:30 before an employee brought Rita's chicken-and-potato dinner to me in the basement. Some nights I didn't stop teaching long enough to eat, and my assistant, Gloria Heiden, would open the folding door to the classroom just wide enough to sneak me a cold drink with only her hand showing. The class would break into uproarious laughter. Like any good straight man, I obliged with a grin and said, "Thanks a cupful, Gloria."

○ ○ ○ ○

Our family grew as quickly as the business. A year and a half after Susan's birth, Nancy was born, and then Paul in 1955. I had thought nothing could take me from my work. But the experience of having three children certainly changed my priorities. I would race upstairs to play with them, feed them, and change their diapers, then run back downstairs for a emergency appointment with a hysterical parent whose concerns I could certainly relate to. Of course, I squeezed in the writing or editing of new lessons. Luckily, it took no time to commute to work. It was all within three stories of my favorite building on Bedford Avenue.

When one lives above the shop, distinctions between family and business fade quickly. My children grew tall enough to reach the doorknobs leading to the basement and wandered in to say "Hi" with a cheerful wave. Lured by the cacophony of classroom sounds, they would stretch their tiny heads around the corner to catch a glimpse of their father lecturing. After a while, I knew there needed to be some separation between home and office, so I implemented the simple solution of raising the doorknobs about twenty inches.

Some evenings I was still in the basement working after the rest of the family had eaten dinner. "Stanley, your dinner's on the table," Rita would call over our intercom.

"Okay, I'm coming," I'd answer.

Ten minutes later she would call more insistently: "Mr. Kaplan, your dinner's getting cold."

Mr. Kaplan? Now I knew she was serious about me getting upstairs in minus two seconds flat.

Five minutes later: "Stanley, your dinner's in the refrigerator," Rita would sigh.

The business was an integral part of our family life, and our family was an even more integral part of our business. I had no objection to nepotism as long as it stayed in the family. My father-in-law became the company accountant and financial adviser whom everyone called Mr. Saul. Rita taught English and did the bookkeeping at our dining room table. My mother wrote the payroll checks from her house every week.

From the very beginning, my family was the central force behind my business, and I wanted them to be part of the growing success because they shared my enthusiasm. And it was always easier, of course, to wake Rita at two in the morning rather than an employee to talk about my teaching ideas. I implicitly trusted my family. They were bright, creative, and ambitious, and I grew to rely on them for every aspect of the operation. There were times, of course, when we didn't see eye to eye, especially when I incessantly pushed my ideas beyond tangible limits. But our differences were overshadowed by the positive results of the growth of my company.

Since his return from military service, my older brother, Sidney, had been tutoring students in foreign languages, math, and English at his home a few miles away. He was a welcome addition when he joined Rita to teach classes in the basement. He worked magic with the students. He had a kind and soft-spoken manner and a wonderful sense of humor. He was a master of puns. "Oops. That was a fluke," he said about a mistake on a practice test that used fishing in a question. When he left to buy gasoline, he gave his class a break and said, "No fueling around." I threatened to send him to a punitentiary for his excessive wordplay.

My father, who was semiretired, still did small plumbing jobs. One of his last jobs was the installation of a new bathroom in our house. It was a godsend to a family with three children and a housekeeper sharing only one bathroom. Soon after, his health began to deteriorate and he died in a Manhattan hospital. It was our first loss of a family member and difficult to accept, especially for my mother. But our family drew closer to fill the gap caused by his absence.

And there was a new generation of Kaplans absorbed into the business as my children grew tall enough to reach the raised doorknobs. Nancy was a born teacher, and as early as age seven she proctored students during the practice tests while wearing her pajamas. She threatened to tell her daddy if anyone cheated. She taught our French housekeeper to read English, creating report cards and adding gold stars where appropriate. Susan, a gifted manager, was put to work cleaning my double-sided blackboard and filing papers. She escorted students to their classes, handed out lesson books, and took attendance. Paul, a whiz with numbers, took control of the ledger by his eighth birthday, filling the pages of a spiral notebook with students' payments and every bank transaction. Paul, bemused by the whole scene, talked a blue streak when he wasn't pushing the pencil on the ledger sheets and sometimes delayed the class lessons by fifteen minutes.

In those early years, the business operated like an insider's club. I wasn't trying to hide my business; quite the opposite. Every successful business needs exposure, but I didn't believe in advertising the business except for a mention in the Yellow Pages. I compared myself to doctors and lawyers, who believed advertising was unprofessional. My best advertisement was a satisfied customer, and I had lots of those.

Savvy Brooklyn mothers who wanted their children to climb the education ladder knew about Kaplan. One mother wanted her straight-A son to have an extra edge, so she brought him to my basement for years for private tutoring in basic subjects. He was extremely bright and today is one of the country's most successful ophthalmologists.

Kaplan also functioned in a behind-the-scenes fashion, because test preparation was not widely accepted. The College Board was telling academics, admissions officers, parents, and students that coaching produced insignificant results and test preparation was a waste of time and money. It was protecting its product by calling my business a hoax and branding me as a charlatan. Soon the academic establishment was calling me a "quack," "the cram king," and a "snake oil salesman." I thought the characterizations were offensive and unfounded. I had established and maintained the highest quality of effective teaching. But there was a bias against my test preparation business because some educators considered a businessman running a private, for-profit company to be a new and dangerous breed in education. I wasn't worried that the name-calling and intolerance would affect my business because students were still flooding through my doors. In fact, I figured such virulent attacks must mean I was doing something right. But I cared about my reputation as a teacher and that the misinformation students received might discourage them from seeking help. One of my students who asked his high school guidance counselor what he could do to improve his SAT score was told, "Nothing." The student heard about my classes from friends and appeared at my basement door the next day.

Students knew that Kaplan courses worked, but educators and test makers continued to think test preparation was tantamount to cheating. I was disappointed and surprised by their reactions. I believed I was offering a quality service the students wanted and needed, so I was disappointed when fellow educators criticized me and excluded me from their meetings.

One evening in 1956, I attended a meeting at a New York public high school where teachers, parents, and students had gathered to talk about an upcoming SAT. I usually didn't go to these meetings, but I was curious to hear what students and parents were being told about the test. The room was crowded when I arrived, and there were only a few vacant seats in the back row of the auditorium. Shortly after I sat down, the teacher addressing the crowd spotted me from the front podium. He stopped in midsentence, pointed his finger directly at me, and exclaimed, "I refuse to continue until THAT MAN leaves the room."

All eyes turned to see the target of the teacher's outburst. To him, my business threatened the role of conventional teaching and education. I was embarrassed by his outburst and a little annoyed, but I stood my ground and stayed while he continued his speech. It was painful to be treated as a pariah, and it didn't help when some parents came over to me after the meeting and patted me on the back in sympathy. I didn't want pity. I was an educator who wanted the respect of the academic establishment. I knew my teaching was helping students, and I wasn't going to stop just because other educators opposed me.

Why was coaching such an anathema? Because test preparation represented a direct challenge to the increasingly powerful College Board. By 1957, half a million students were taking the SAT, and coaching tutors were expanding their roles in direct proportion to the popularity of the SAT. The College Board did not like having its authority questioned. It feared that if coaching worked, some students would have an unfair advantage on a test that was supposed to measure everyone equally. That threatened the quality of its product.

I had no desire to discredit the College Board or invalidate the SAT. In fact, I believed that the SAT, when used in conjunction with grades, was an effective instrument in predicting academic success. Coaching simply helped students become better students. If students improved their SAT scores, the scores were an indicator of their improved ability, not an inflated result. I felt that coaching strengthened, rather than weakened, the validity of the SAT, because students were performing at their true potential. I might have been accepted to medical school if I had been able to display my true potential to admissions officials.

For one fleeting moment in 1957, the College Board changed its position on coaching. In that year, the Board issued a new SAT handbook that gave a tepid endorsement to long-term preparation. "If coaching means an honest effort, under the guidance of a good teacher, over an extended period of time, to improve those skills in which you are weak, then it can be recommended as effective study," the handbook stated. "But coaching courses or coaching schools which promise to give you a collection of nuggets of fact, or to provide intensive drill with sample questions that will 'assure your success,' are not worth your time and money." Also in 1957, students for the first time could receive their own SAT scores—a major step forward.

But the College Board's grudging advocacy didn't last long. A few years later, the Board reverted to its prior language once it realized that its statement might encourage a proliferation of coaching schools. The College Board faced increased competition from other test makers, and it couldn't afford to have its tests weakened. It was particularly sensitive to the presence of a new competitor, the American College Testing Program (ACT), founded at the University of Iowa to provide a college admission exam primarily for midwestern and California public colleges and universities. The ACT was becoming the test that most midwestern high school students took for college placement. Eventually many schools throughout the nation began accepting either the SAT or ACT for admission, and today almost as many students take the ACT as the SAT.

The College Board's reputation hinged on the constancy, reliability, and validity of its tests and on the credibility of the ETS, the College Board organization that created and administered the SAT and other standardized tests. If the College Board believed that test preparation undermined those features, it had no choice but to oppose coaching. The College Board knew it was imperative to convince academics, guidance counselors, parents, and students that its product was sound and impervious to outside influences.

But the College Board's claims didn't curb students' appetite for coaching. Enrollment at my center was growing, not shrinking, and I wasn't even staging a loud counterargument against the anticoaching position. I didn't see a need to. Scoring well on this test was becoming important, and students and parents knew I could help. Others began offering test preparation too, although on a much smaller scale than my school offered. A group of high school teachers, principals, and school superintendents who understood the benefits of test preparation moonlighted on the side to coach students for the SAT.

But even as test preparation proliferated and Kaplan enrollment soared, I often wondered if this was a short-lived opportunity. What if the demand was a temporary fluke? Would my business be successful five years down the road? What if the College Board decided to discontinue using the SAT? What if parents and students began to buy the line that test preparation was a hoax? I didn't conduct any fancy market surveys to direct my business decisions; I just responded to the demand. And as long as it was steady, I continued to thrive. So I had to continue to believe in myself and in the quality and effectiveness of my services. There was always a demand for good tutors, and if the SAT business fell off, I could always return to preparing students for the Regents and basic studies. I might have been a young, inexperienced businessman, but I was a strong and confident teacher.

BOO: BOO: BOO: $\sqrt{2}$:
SOME LESSONS YOU NEVER FORGET

I was walking along Fifth Avenue in New York City a few years ago when a man called to me, "Boo: Boo: Boo: $\sqrt{2}$." Most people would have thought he was crazy, but I stopped and smiled. "You're Stanley Kaplan!" the man said. "I took your course forty years ago in the basement of your home, and I still remember Boo: Boo: Boo: $\sqrt{2}$."

In the early days of our SAT preparation, my brother Sidney and I used to concoct silly games, funny names, and endless puns to make learning fun. This stimulated our students to think and helped them understand and remember the concepts we were teaching.

"Boo: Boo: Boo: $\sqrt{2}$" was a catchy formula I taught students to help them remember the Pythagorean theorem when applied to an isosceles right triangle. This triangle has two equal sides—or legs—that meet at a 90-degree angle. The third side of the triangle, opposite the right angle, is called the hypotenuse. Devised by the Greek philosopher Pythagoras in the sixth century B.C., the Pythagorean theorem states that the sum of the squares of the lengths of the sides of a right triangle is equal to the square of the length of the hypotenuse ($a^2 + b^2 = c^2$). That was pretty confusing, but knowing it was imperative, because the theorem appeared in numerous applications on the SAT. Today the theorem is printed at the beginning of the SAT math section, so students do not need to memorize it, but they still need to know how to apply it. To help my students remember the theorem without wasting valuable time during the test, I created ways to help students apply the theorem. For instance, I assigned the silly name Boo to each side of an isosceles right triangle. To find the length of the hypotenuse, the students only needed to multiply the length of a leg (or Boo) by $\sqrt{2}$, or 1.41. All they had to remember was Boo: Boo: Boo: $\sqrt{2}$. That always got a laugh from the students, and when they saw a question using the theorem on the test, they remembered my lesson and got the correct answer quickly.

But Boo: Boo: Boo: $\sqrt{2}$ applied only to an isosceles right triangle. So I taught them many other quick tricks to apply the theorem to right triangles without sides of equal length. For instance, I would draw a diagram like this one:

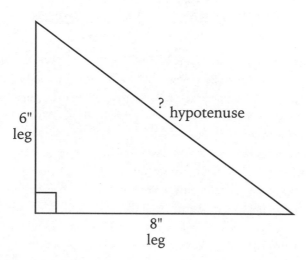

I told them 6 squared was 36, and 8 squared was 64. Those lengths added together equal 100, or the length of the hypotenuse squared. The square root of 100 is 10 and the correct answer to the question. As you can see, there is a sequence in the ratio of the lengths of the sides. In this case, the sequence is 6, 8, 10. If a question asked for the hypotenuse of a triangle with sides measuring 5 and 7 inches, the student immediately knew without calculations that the answer had to be less than 10, because 5 is less than 6 and 7 is less than 8 (the answer is 8.6 inches to be exact). I instructed students that one of the choices given on the test will be the exact answer, so in this example they should choose the answer closest to 9 inches.

Some students, however, neglected to apply their knowledge of the theorem to a practical situation, and got "hung up" on a question about a coat hanger's measurements. The test question asked students to calculate the distance between the base of the hook and the midpoint of the base. It looked like this:

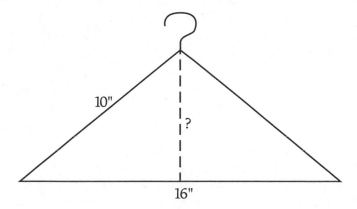

To find the answer, draw a dotted line *(x)* from the bottom of the hook to the base of the triangle. We now have a right triangle with one leg of 8 and a hypotenuse of 10. Using the famous 6, 8, 10 right triangle sequence, *x* must be equal to 6.

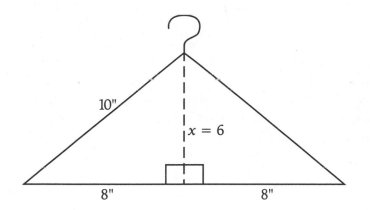

After the test, some students came back to me and said, "We never had coat hanger questions in class. We didn't know to use the Pythagorean theorem." Unfortunately, these students had simply memorized information without applying their knowledge to solve the problem.

It was a good example to show students that they could think out a problem, instead of depending on memorization. I'll never forget when a student named Debbie discovered thinking. She had scored poorly on her PSAT and had a slim chance of getting into her first-choice college without a good SAT score even though her GPA was a 3.6. She enrolled in my SAT classes and I was amazed by her steady gains. I asked her, "What's your secret?" I still remember her answer: "Mr. Kaplan, before now I never thought of thinking." What a novel idea—thinking! She had always relied on memorizing information but now realized this was not enough. She epitomized my raison d'être. She called me after receiving her SAT scores to tell me her score had jumped more than 500 points. She attended the University of Chicago, made the dean's list every year, and subsequently earned a Ph.D. in clinical psychology. Her ability to reason and solve problems made all the difference in her life.

It was important to me to know that my teaching was effective with other students as well, so my students reported their PSAT and SAT scores to us, and we kept meticulous records to track their gains from test to test. Most took the SAT more than once, before and after coaching. We discovered that the average score improvement exceeded 100 points, and some students achieved score increases in the range of 250 points. We also substantiated these improvements with the diagnostic tests we gave students during classes. We could tell we were doing something right because most students improved their scores. Critics challenged our significant levels of improvement, but Kaplan students and their parents knew the secret behind the increased scores: that hard work with superior study materials and teachers could yield dramatic results. Most students who attended all the classes, completed the weekly homework, and listened to the Test-N-Tape review would learn the subject matter and how to apply the concepts.

Not all students, however, improved their scores, and we offered no guarantees. If a high school junior read at a seventh-grade level, a ten-week SAT course could do little to raise that student's scores to an acceptable level. It was the avid readers, the ones who had been studying since childhood, who scored high on both the verbal and math sections. The motivated students always improved the most. When parents asked me when a student should begin preparing for admissions tests, I always answered, "In kindergarten" or "Three years ago." My answer was partly tongue in cheek, but my point was that it's never too early to start reading and developing good study skills. My message was: Start early.

One trademark of my teaching was close interaction with students. Their scholastic performance was my utmost responsibility. The best teachers connect with their students. I learned all my students' names by playing a memory game. While a student answered a question, I silently repeated the name until I could address each student. I learned about my students' hobbies and experiences. Once I had gained a student's respect and confidence, I had him or her in my corner. My students told me that I was different from their teachers in school. I was their coach, their cheerleader. I was "Stan the Man." One former student told me, "You were our first academic coach. You gave us the tools to do well on this exam in a finite period of time and showed us how to organize and focus. You made us set goals and achieve them."

I liked to interact with my students and reward their hard work. In the late 1950s, I began hosting "TGIO—Thank Goodness It's Over" celebration parties after the SAT. "Come celebrate with your fellow classmates and teachers for having survived E-Day (Exam Day)." My students washed down hot dogs, sandwiches, and pizza with root beer and Cokes. The atmosphere was festive, and, of course, everyone talked about the SAT that they had taken just hours before.

"What did you think about that question to compute the fraction of acid when mixed with a certain amount of water?" one student would ask another.

Students might recall ten versions of the same question, but what was important was that they understood the concepts involved. One student told us that the vocabulary word "fillip" had been on the test. I had never heard that word before. Now my students were teaching me.

I could tell from their conversations what the SAT must have been like without having seen it myself. I learned about the test's length, structure, and subject matter. After the students left, my staff and I would recall the students' conversations and write different practice questions using the same types of questions. My students would then be prepared for any question on a specific topic without knowing the exact test question.

When my staff and I wrote practice questions, we added personal details for fun, such as the names of my children, my wife, my friends' children, and my nieces and nephews. I had a big enough family that we had an ample supply of names. Good thing, because over the years I wrote thousands of these questions.

Although I had the College Board sample questions as a guide for creating practice tests and study material, I still felt I was dangling my fishing pole in a pool of murky water, never knowing where the fish might be biting. I was trying to teach students how to take a test I had never seen—a test that was, in many ways, as alien as a distant planet.

I spent hours trying to understand the design of the test, trying to think like the test makers, anticipating the types of questions my students would face. How could students be required to take a test without knowing what was expected of them? To me, the College Board's practice of giving students limited information about the test was unfair. Of course, students shouldn't see the actual test beforehand, but they should be informed about what types of general math and verbal skills they are required to know. If what the College Board said were true—that the test measured abilities developed over time and could not be coached—then supplying the nature, layout, and format of the questions beforehand could not be viewed as cheating or eroding the validity of the test. The College Board's method didn't empower students; it deprived them of their right to be fully informed. And they should have been able to see their graded tests along with their scores. After all, the New York Board of Regents had made a mistake in computing my scores, and if I hadn't complained I would have been denied a scholarship. If the SAT had an ambiguous question, students had the right to double-check their answers and scores.

The pizza parties became quite popular, but one Brooklyn high school principal called the College Board's ETS and said I was asking each student to memorize questions from the test and report back to me. Of course, this accusation was false. The principal was accusing me of using my students to cheat and steal questions. I would never steal questions from a test. That would be cheating my students out of an education, and I would never cheat or steal to advance my business. Did the College Board assume that half a million students took the SAT each year without talking about it afterward and that nobody would be listening?

In fact, I told my students at the first class, "If anybody is here because they expect to find questions that will appear on the test, then go to the desk and ask for a full tuition refund, because that's not what you'll get here. We're trying to develop concepts, not just spoon-feed questions that might appear on the examinations." And I never instructed my students to memorize questions. "You're in this test for you, and it's unethical to copy questions."

I remembered my college zoology professor, Dr. Bayliss, who announced on the first day of class that he was giving us the questions that would be on his tests during the semester. We smiled and thought, "This will be an easy A." Then Dr. Bayliss gave us a list of four hundred questions, and we quickly realized that learning the answers meant learning everything about zoology. He taught to the test, and we learned zoology. I was teaching to the test too, but not by giving out actual questions or teaching students to memorize answers.

Meanwhile, the work conditions in the basement were worsening. Students and staff were crammed into every nook and cranny, the bookshelves groaned under the weight of study materials, and students bickered over who could listen to tapes next.

Space was becoming such a problem that I rented a small, dank classroom in the basement of a local church to accommodate extra students. But I was embarrassed by the decrepit conditions, which appeared so unprofessional.

"Help!" I cried one day into the phone to my attorney. "I need more space. The basement is bursting at its seams. And I'm teaching students in an annex that looks like a dungeon." I told him that I had found a new place to rent, a podiatrist's home office on East Seventeenth Street near Kings Highway at the Brighton Beach subway stop. It was a great location and much cheaper than commercial space. But it was zoned residential. My attorney shrewdly advised me to remove the kitchen, thereby creating a non-residential space to meet the zoning laws. I took his advice and opened my first center away from my home. Now I was in business. The new location was near the bustling Kings Highway shopping district and one block from the subway train that connected my school to Brooklyn and beyond. Parents from Long Island would drop off their children at my center and then spend hours shopping along Kings Highway. Within a few months, an appreciative Kings Highway Chamber of Commerce invited me to become a member, and a year later I was made a vice president.

A sign over the front door read, "Stanley H. Kaplan Educational Center." Inside was a combined office and reception area with a Coke machine that dispensed free drinks from revolving slots for the staff. There were two classrooms, and the former kitchen was transformed into a tape room stocked with hundreds of tapes. Students wearing chunky earphones sat hunched over tape recorders to hear my math tips or funny anecdotes about vocabulary words. Students snickered as my voice intoned, "I know you like the idea of turning me off, but go back and listen to that last question."

Another room was used exclusively for printing. I bought a duplicating machine called the Gestetner, recently developed in Great Britain based on the first stencil duplicator patented by Thomas Edison. Compared with today's copying equipment, the process was archaic even though it was then the most advanced system available. The text was typed on wax-coated stencils that ripped easily, and I thought one of my receptionists would quit when she had to retype the same page four times. Once the stencil was clamped and turned on a hand-cranked cylinder, purple ink oozed from the stencil cuts onto paper. Some copies were then dried on a clothesline strung across the former kitchen, and the pungent smell of ink and paper wafted through the classroom. The clothesline blocked traffic, but it was convenient once classes began because we simply snatched the copies off the line and handed them to students.

Every night I stayed up past midnight writing new questions and study materials. My assistants would groan when I appeared the next day with revisions or additions, because it meant preparing a new stencil and cranking out new copies. The clack, clack, clack of typewriter keys sounded as my staff busily prepared new tests.

Typists and technical aides produced voluminous packets of my study materials, all stamped with the slogan "AS DEVELOPED BY STANLEY H. KAPLAN" that signified the unique quality of the work. I gave staff and students custom-made T-shirts proclaiming: "SUCCESS THROUGH EDUCATION AS DEVELOPED BY STANLEY H. KAPLAN."

One handout with tips on using word roots for definitions began, "GET TO THE ROOT OF THE MATTER! inCREDible, CREDible, CREDential, CREDulous, CREDence." Another math tip was "ESTIMATE WHEN POSSIBLE." For example, since 12 divided by 3 equals 4, then 12 divided by 3.14 is a value slightly less than 4. That's usually close enough to select the right choice without long, time-consuming calculations. I ended a tip sheet with this advice: "WHEN-EVER YOU HAVE EXCLUDED THE IMPOSSIBLE, WHATEVER REMAINS, HOWEVER IMPROBABLE, MUST BE THE TRUTH—SHERLOCK HOLMES."

For years I relied on Rita and Sidney to supplement my teaching. But as enrollment grew, I hired teachers to give myself more time to write study materials and practice tests. I chose dynamic, crackerjack teachers and I ex-pected them to expostulate, gesticulate, ham it up, and keep students on their toes. The first interview question for prospective teachers was "What was your SAT score?" If they said 1400 or above, that meant they were crit-ical thinkers and understood the test. I also required them to take one of my diagnostic SAT tests to see if their skills were still sharp. If they passed muster, a lengthy interview followed. An appreciation of my sense of humor always earned them extra points.

The quality of teaching was a crucial element in the success of my school. The teacher set the class tone and was the key element of a student's performance. Kaplan teachers were expected to deliver lessons with the same fervor and clarity as I did. I trained them with audiotapes and even suggested they borrow some of my funniest classroom jokes.

I expected my teachers to dress professionally in suits, ties, jackets, and dresses. Most complied. One hip teacher, however, repeatedly revealed her midriff and was constantly chided by my staff. "You must cover your navel, Miss Young," they warned her. So Miss Young had to borrow a sweater or jacket before each class began.

I had so many students now that I discontinued my individual tutoring except in a few special cases. Most students now wanted SAT and Regents preparation, and I discovered that they learned just as well, if not better, in a group. They listened to one another's questions and found it was more fun to study together than alone. It was also less expensive for them than private tutoring. If students needed extra work or individual attention, they could come to me for help or listen to specific review tapes. I reduced my SAT course from sixteen classes to ten, which cost $150. Each four-hour class was held once a week. Ten weeks seemed the best length of time for students to avoid losing the edge and enthusiasm they needed on test day.

My center became informally known as Kaplan Kollege, and the students were Kaplanites. I induced more giggles, guffaws, and chuckles during classes than a comedian at a Catskills nightclub. "Here's an example to tickle your brain," I told the students. "Thirteen people are in a Great Neck restaurant eating salami sandwiches. Ten people are eating pickles. Six are eating both sandwiches and pickles. How many people are eating just a pickle or a sandwich?" One of my better students thrust his hand high in the air and shouted, "Seventeen."

"Hah. Your answer comes from not thinking this out," I responded. "You added thirteen and ten and then subtracted six." Then I drew two big intersecting circles on the blackboard. "But if six people are eating *both* salami sandwiches and pickles"—and I filled in the intersection of the circles with chalk—"then seven are eating only salami sandwiches and four are eating only pickles." While I talked, I drew seven Xs in one circle to denote the sandwich eaters and four Xs in the other circle for the pickle eaters. "That makes eleven people eating just a pickle or a sandwich.

"We all know that the only people who would eat a salami sandwich without a pickle are superschmoes," I continued, "and anyone sitting in a restaurant eating only pickles is a schlemiel. And you might argue with the test makers that that many superschmoes and schlemiels can't be found in a Great Neck restaurant, but that still won't make your answer right."

When students scored 650 or higher on the SAT, I awarded them a certificate and inducted them into the "Phi Beta Kaplan" society. If they raised their score by 150 points or more, I gave them SHK monogrammed sweatshirts. In one class, all eighteen students received sweatshirts. And I still dispensed the dimes, quarters, and half dollars to students who correctly answered the tough questions. Sometimes I had a class with very bright students and gave away coins so quickly that I had to send a staff member to the bank for extra rolls of coins or issue IOUs. It was the best financial investment I could have made.

BEATING A PATH TO MY DOORSTEP

It was the 1960s, and times were changing. Across the nation, especially on college campuses, people were demanding racial, gender, and economic equality. America had led the world in promoting public education, and now the nation looked to its institutions of learning to be vanguards in the movement toward social justice. The public was asking: Why weren't more minorities and economically disadvantaged students attending Harvard or other highly selective colleges? Why weren't more universities better integrated? If education was a door to success, why not fling open the campus gates wider and admit qualified students regardless of gender, creed, or color?

Public demand prompted changes. The Ivy League colleges, despite resistance and delays, instituted more liberal admissions policies to diversify their student bodies. For the first time, Yale admitted students regardless of their ability to pay. America was building a system of an academic meritocracy with a foundation of talent, not privilege.

At the same time, America was suffering from an inferiority complex about the country's quality of education. After the Russians launched the *Sputnik* spacecraft in 1957, Americans pushed for better technological competency and higher standards in education. States expanded their higher education systems to accommodate more students and offered free or reduced tuition for their residents. The economy was booming, and enrollment in the nation's public higher education institutions more than tripled. It was a prime time for an increased reliance on standardized tests.

As they had after World War II, colleges and universities depended on standardized admissions tests—primarily the SAT and the ACT—to handle the influx of admissions applications. And they also began using test scores on a regular basis to promote their academic quality or ranking. "The average SAT score of our admitting class is 1300," some schools bragged.

Schools were giving test scores greater weight in the application process. One of my former students was accepted by a top-rate university because his improved SAT scores carried him over the top. "The major factors in our final decision to extend an offer of admission to you at this time were your strong performance to date in your senior courses, and your just received November SAT scores, indicating dramatic increases in your scores, particularly in the verbal areas," an admissions director wrote to the student in a letter. "We were deeply concerned by your original verbal score, but your current score is certainly far more within our expectation, and coupled with the nature of your total academic record . . . enables us to extend, with confidence, an offer of admission to you."

But in a climate of protests and sit-ins against academic and government institutions, students questioned the authority of the test makers and the importance placed on test scores. Their scrutiny was valid, but I also pointed out to them how standardized tests could help. I still supported the use of admissions tests along with grades as the best predictors of success because grade inflation was rampant. I asked my students, "How many of you like the SAT?" Not a single hand was raised. "But you should like the SAT," I told them. "If you have a low GPA or attended a poor-quality high school, the SAT can change the reputation that precedes you." My students now included minorities and women, a drastic change from the predominantly white male students I had taught during the 1940s and 1950s. I told them there was no universal measuring tool when I had applied to medical school and that they were fortunate to be judged by uniform assessment.

But mine was a qualified endorsement. Too much reliance on standardized tests creates an arbitrary system of judging by numbers. Scores must be used in conjunction with a personal interview and a student's GPA—which is the best barometer of a student's ability to accomplish a task over a long period of time. It takes more than good test scores to be a successful student, and standardized tests do not measure academic discipline, motivation, or creativity.

By the 1960s, most high school students were taking the SAT or ACT for college admission, but other tests were introduced as well. The College Board created the Preliminary Scholastic Aptitude Test (PSAT) to familiarize students with the SAT format. Students came to my center seeking PSAT test preparation, and I was eager to accommodate them. I also received requests to prepare for the ACT, and it was easy to adapt my teaching methods to any test.

At the same time, the requests for SAT preparation surged, and students who traveled from all over the New York metropolitan area to Brooklyn now wanted me to come to them. In 1961, a former SAT student called me and said his younger brother wanted to take a Kaplan SAT course. "How about coming out to Great Neck in Long Island? We're not in Timbuktu," he said. "We have a big home where you can teach. We won't charge you rent, and we'll give you all the Cokes you can drink. I guarantee you'll have ten of his friends to teach as well."

"Twenty-five?" I suggested.

"You've got it," he said.

I agreed and drove my Mercury sedan filled with books and tapes to his parents' home each week. The classes were a huge success and all but one of the students were accepted to Ivy League schools. During a second round of classes in Great Neck, a hundred students showed up. Soon I was traveling all over the metropolitan area to teach SAT classes and renting space in churches, synagogues, and schools for my classrooms.

But the largest number of new requests for test preparation came from former SAT students who were now in college and wanted help with graduate and professional school admissions exams. The two most popular requests were preparation for the Law School Admission Test (LSAT) and the Medical College Admission Test (MCAT).

The MCAT was—and still is—a very difficult exam. It is given by the Association of American Medical Colleges (AAMC) for acceptance to medical school and tests students on basic sciences, including biology, organic and inorganic chemistry, and physics.

To my knowledge, I was the first person in the test preparation industry to teach MCAT classes. In fact, I remember the first time we received a call from a student wanting help with the MCAT. My assistant who answered the phone came to me and whispered, "What's the MCAT?"

"It's the test I never had," I answered.

Now I had a new challenge. As with the SAT, I had never seen the MCAT. So I began talking to my former SAT and Regents students who were now in medical school and had taken the MCAT. I also studied the MCAT instruction booklet all students received before taking the test. All of this gave me a fair idea of what the MCAT was like. I could tell it was not an easy test and it wouldn't be easy to prepare students to take it.

Once I understood the test and its guidelines, I was able to create a verisimilar test as a practice tool. I hired medical students to help me write study materials and sample tests. Within six months, we were ready for our first class. It was attended by six premed college students, all of whom had taken a Kaplan SAT class. When the course was finished, we celebrated with a helluva party.

Then came a flood of premed students looking for MCAT preparation. I hired interns and medical students, those who had scored high on their MCATs, to teach more classes and write study materials and practice tests. They were perfect candidates for the job, because they were only a couple of years older than our students and they possessed a crisp and current knowledge of the material and the tests. Most of them were former Kaplan students, so I knew their strengths and abilities as teachers and researchers.

MCAT students began their preparation program fifteen weeks in advance of the test to cover the two hundred hours of material we provided. That included forty hours of class sessions and additional hours devoted to proctored practice tests, supplementary study materials, and review tapes. Some students preferred to use tapes rather than attend class because they could absorb the complex material at their own pace any time of day or night.

It was a challenge preparing students for this rigorous and demanding daylong exam. One former student wanted to attend medical school ten years after graduating from college. When she arrived at my center, I gave her a diagnostic test to assess her skills, and her low score prompted a torrent of tears. "I think I left nine answers blank for every one I answered," she sobbed. "I feel like I have only an eighth-grade education."

I consoled her and pointed out how tough the MCAT was. I explained that even though she had been a good student, she needed lots of review, and she needed to sharpen her problem-solving skills. She worked hard in my class, and gradually her skills improved. Months after she took the

MCAT, I received a letter of thanks from her. She had scored above average on her MCAT, had been accepted into medical school, and was on her way to fulfilling her dream.

The Law School Admission Test, or LSAT, was in some respects the most crucial of all exams in the admissions process. The LSAT was mandatory for admission to law school, and most law schools imposed a minimum LSAT score threshold for admission. Because law schools use a complicated formula combining the GPA and LSAT scores, the LSAT carried more weight than other admissions tests. A student's GPA cannot be dramatically improved after his or her junior year of college, so the LSAT score was the only critical factor in the formula that could improve a student's overall admissions portfolio. Also, if a student took the LSAT more than once, the scores were averaged instead of using only the highest single score. That meant that scoring well on every LSAT taken was imperative. All these conditions made preparing for the LSAT even more important.

The LSAT emphasized strong verbal and logical reasoning skills. The early LSAT had some math and vocabulary, but the test concentrated on reading comprehension, reasoning, and verbal brainpower. So we targeted these areas. I told my students during their first LSAT class, "Don't worry if you didn't score well on the SAT. It didn't brand you as an intellectual ignoramus for the rest of your life. You might have been a little pipsqueak in high school, didn't care about learning, weren't motivated to study, never read. But you matured in college and did much better. I'm sure you'll do better on the LSAT."

Student demand for LSAT preparation became so pervasive in the 1960s that new test preparation companies came out of the woodwork to specialize in only LSAT preparation. One of these was founded by John Sexton, a Brooklyn Catholic school teacher who first started his company to raise money for his students' debate team. He later sold his company and today is the president of New York University. Test preparation competition had increased over the years, and although some new, smaller companies were giving us a run for our money, we still held the largest market share and there was enough LSAT preparation business to spread around.

Kaplan offered preparation classes for the SAT, PSAT, ACT, LSAT, and MCAT. And the acronyms of other postgraduate admissions tests were surfacing like noodles in alphabet soup: GRE (Graduate Record Examination, for graduate school). GMAT (Graduate Management Admission Test), and DAT (Dental Admission Test). Of course, we were quick to introduce preparation classes for each test. My staff and I simply replicated the successful teaching methods we used in SAT preparation—classes, homework, tapes, and practice tests—and tailored the contents to each specific course. I was becoming a distinguished man of letters: SAT, DAT, GMAT, GRE, MCAT, LSAT.

The nation's increasing reliance on admissions tests was a boon for test makers too. By now the ETS unabashedly called itself the "world's gatekeeper." The ETS administered not only the SAT and PSAT but also fifteen achievement tests in a variety of subjects used by almost eight hundred colleges. Almost two million students were taking ETS-created tests each year. The ETS held the academic future of millions of people in its hands, and its tests were used for screening everything from golf pros to real estate agents. Any doubts about test validity or scrutiny of ETS operations could erode public confidence in this powerful organization. And a loss of public trust could threaten the viability of its products.

So it was not surprising that the College Board and the ETS lashed out to discredit coaching companies, or "cram schools," as the College Board called them. An ETS director's report stated, "If the College Board's tests can be beaten through coaching, then the Board is itself discredited." Yet more tests brought more coaching. More coaching brought more College Board resistance. It issued virulent disclaimers, saying it was "appalled by the subversive effect of these commercial enterprises on the goals of education." I don't think the College Board ever anticipated that coaching would emerge as such a persistent and pervasive threat to its integrity. Ironically, its own resistance to coaching seemed to fuel the debate and prompt more public scrutiny. But the College Board was trying to protect its organization and preserve its reputation.

In 1965, the College Board published its most forceful opposition in a little green book called *The Effects of Coaching on Scholastic Aptitude Test Scores*. The "green book," as it was dubbed, didn't mince words. It stated emphatically that seven studies (four conducted by the College Board and three by independent researchers) had proved that short-term coaching was unnecessary and ill advised. The green book said that coaching produced such small benefits that students should not waste their time and money on it. Years later, the green book would be discredited by researchers for making selective omissions when summarizing the studies and for omitting other studies that said that coaching seemed to work. If it had included my students in a study, I could have proven categorically that coaching helped.

Coaching had never enjoyed a good reputation in academic circles, but now the College Board was referring to "coaching" as if it were a dirty eight-letter word. Critics in established academia described coaching as "clandestine" because classes were held in hotels, homes, and basements. One College Board spokesman said on national television that he would never send his daughter to test prep courses because they exploited students' anxieties and were ineffective. Some admissions officers told me they would shave points off a student's application or reject it altogether if they learned a student had taken my courses. Students told me that counselors had advised them not to take a test prep class because they might be penalized in the application process. Test prep was so taboo that some students enrolled anonymously and paid with cash. Never before had I had so many students named Jane Doe and Albert Einstein!

The attacks on test preparation and my company were unjust. The College Board was unfair to give students misleading information about the effects of coaching. My center was a reputable place of learning that helped students, and I wanted Kaplan to have the sterling image it deserved. I told students and parents to ignore the disclaimers, because they had every right to get extra help. I urged parents to complain to school officials about the misinformation, and some of them did. But I never called or visited the College Board or the ETS to directly challenge the message about coaching because I was certain that their position was untenable, and I thought it would be short-lived.

Ironically, the College Board message about coaching either was not heard or was ignored by many because my business was booming. One heavily traveled path for many Brooklyn children was Kaplan, then Cornell, Yale, or the University of Michigan. Taking a Kaplan class became a rite of passage for middle-class kids who wanted to go to competitive schools.

They passed the word to younger siblings and friends, and local schools, clubs, and temples began listing my class schedules in their newsletters.

One student wanted to attend my classes so badly he came to me on the sly against his parents' wishes. He said they didn't understand how competitive it was to get into college in the 1960s, and he secretly enrolled in my classes with money he earned as a paperboy. He increased his SAT score by 340 points after taking my course and was accepted to a highly selective college in upstate New York. Today he has a Ph.D. in physics and is a scientist at Xerox Corporation.

And his parents? He eventually told them he was attending my classes and even converted the whole family to Kaplan. I hired his mother as a receptionist, and she later enrolled her daughter in my SAT classes.

We worked hard to promote Kaplan and convert skeptics. One of my enterprising employees, Lucille San Giorgio, was a Kaplan booster who believed in our product and decided to make a soft sell to Catholic schools even though the staff at many private schools were reticent toward preparation. Some private schools were so anti–test prep that they forbade test preparation outside school. They felt it undermined the reputation of their teachers, who led small classes and emphasized math and verbal skills. Yet Lucille's credible, persistent approach won over many of these schools. When we showed them that our classes supplemented, not replaced, their own classroom instruction, they invited us to teach test preparation classes in their schools. That became a new marketing approach for us.

It also marked the beginning of our effort to forge new relationships with school administrators, teachers, and counselors. Of course, some would never waiver in their belief that Kaplan stood for nothing more than reputable cheating. But we persisted in arguing that we could help their students. Some counselors and teachers realized the value of preparation and secretly advised students to take my SAT course with the caveat that they tell no one. Some advisers pretended outwardly that prep courses wouldn't help but privately turned to me and said, "I know the course helps."

We also reached out to the neighborhood yeshivas. For years these Jewish schools had sent their students to Kaplan to study for the Regents exams, and now they wanted their students to have SAT preparation too. A favorite memory was when I prepared students from a Brooklyn yeshiva for the SAT. The students were bright and articulate, but because their teachers had not emphasized a secular curriculum, the students needed help preparing for the SAT. When they appeared at my school on Fridays, I assumed for weeks that the yeshiva was dismissed for the day. But one Friday the students beat a rapid exit from my class when someone shouted, "The principal's coming!" In walked the yeshiva principal, looking for his students, who were cutting their Friday yeshiva classes to attend mine.

A negative side effect of the growing importance of admissions tests was anxiety. For many students, test day meant doomsday. The mere mention of the three seemingly innocent letters—S-A-T—incited sweating, gasping, groaning, and swooning. Adding the L to SAT only worsened the symptoms. One twenty-year-old student whom I prepared for the LSAT was so nervous that his mother accompanied him to class armed with a supply of terry-cloth towels. She stood outside the classroom and when he emerged from our class sessions dripping in sweat, she wiped him dry and then nudged him back into the classroom.

A twelve-year-old student so loathed his tests at school that he would become physically ill. His father sought help from a psychiatrist, who recommended I be part of a team to help the boy. Instilling confidence was my principal aim. We talked, joked, answered questions in his workbook, and, most important, took practice tests. His teachers gave me his tests to administer at his home. One day I said, "Tell your teacher you're ready to take a test with the other students," and I sent him back to the classroom. He insisted on taking the SAT and MCAT on his own and eventually became a physician in Brooklyn.

There's a poignant side note to this story. While I was tutoring this boy, my daughter Nancy developed pneumonia, and her condition turned critical. I called the boy's father, who was a physician, at midnight. He rushed to our house, wrapped Nancy in a blanket, and drove her to the hospital, where she recovered. Rita and I were forever grateful.

I could wallpaper the walls of my classrooms with letters from students who thought they were poor test takers. Students were baffled over why they received high grades in school and then bombed on an admissions test. Almost all "terrible test takers" have two common features: a high anxiety level and a lack of knowledge about the subject matter and mechanics of the test. A good test taker is a student who scores as well as possible given his or her educational background and state of preparedness.

I treated anxiety by instilling confidence, which comes from familiarity with the test. The greatest fears spring from the unknown. If students know what to expect, the tests are no longer growling monsters. No surprises, no anxieties. With a little tender loving care, gentle prodding, and practice, most students went into the tests cool and confident. Then they could focus and perform their best.

"Mr. Kaplan, I was so nervous when I walked in," a student once told me. "But after the first two minutes I calmed down and I could take it because it was just like your practice tests." I was not called the Test Doctor for nothing.

It was natural for parents and students to be concerned about test performance. After all, these tests were important milestones in the life of anyone who wanted a college or postgraduate education. I wanted my students to do the very best possible, but I tried to calm their fears by reminding them that 95 percent of the students who apply to colleges and universities are accepted. "You may not get your first choice, but there's always a college you can attend," I reassured them. The highest SAT scores were necessary only for admission to the top one hundred highly selective schools in America. One of my former students scored 1400 on her SAT but took my courses to get an even better score. She was reaching for the brass ring. And she took home the top prize: the highest possible score, 1600.

Students were not the only ones who learned to relax and answer questions while the clock ticked. One of my employees, Bob Verini, remained so cool under pressure that he won $100,000 in the 1987 Jeopardy Tournament of Champions. Three years later the tournament champions were reunited, and he came in second with a $50,000 purse. Of course, he was exceedingly smart and a voracious reader and loved trivia, but he also had lots of help from my staff throwing questions at him to prepare for his big television quiz show appearances.

I was often accused by admissions counselors of advancing my business by preying on students' anxieties. But I didn't create the anxieties, I just tried to ease them. How does a student feel when the local newspaper refers to the forthcoming SAT as the "Saturday Morning Massacre"? Or the child of a parent who insists that Johnny achieve a certain score or be grounded? I heard one father brag to another parent about his son: " 'We' got into Harvard." Now, that's pressure! I knew a strapping athlete who became physically ill before taking the SAT because his mother was so demanding. Another mother called me and said, "Mr. Kaplan, I think I'm going to commit suicide. My son made only a 1000 on the SAT." She was going to commit suicide over her son's test score? Obviously this was hyperbole, but maybe he had scored poorly because the parental pressure and expectations were just too great.

Parents are a child's first teacher, and educational institutions are no substitute for parental influence. Children are keenly aware of their parents' expectations, demands, and praise. When a parent is stressed about a test, so is the child. I told parents not to make unreasonable demands. Striving for perfection is a virtue, but not at the expense of a child's self-esteem or happiness. I advised parents not to use test scores to measure their children's worth. Test scores are only one indicator of ability and do not always correlate with long-term academic or intellectual performance. A child's success in the long run depends on many factors that cannot be quantitatively measured by tests.

Not wanting to be the shoemaker whose children had no shoes, I tried to help my own children with their ABCs. After the last of my students went home, I would trudge upstairs to my children's rooms to help them with their homework. I felt I was never a good enough teacher for them, but I tried my best. Sometimes their desire to "catch on" quickly got in the way of the learning process. Sometimes there were tears, but mostly the broad smiles that success brings.

I was so busy working on weekends and in the evenings that I tried to reserve Wednesdays for my family—"Wonderful Wednesdays," I called them. Rita and I would pile the children into the Mercury convertible, prop a bulky reel-to-reel tape recorder on the front seat, and plug its power cord into the cigarette lighter. The Kaplan family left Brooklyn with the car top down, children hanging out the sides, and the sounds of Mozart, Beethoven, or our favorite show tunes blaring. "Mozart was a famous German composer and musician who wrote his first oratorio when he was ten years old," I told the children. They stared at me wide-eyed. They were the only children in the neighborhood with taped music in their car.

One of our family's favorite places to visit on "Wonderful Wednesday" was the construction site of the Verrazano Narrows Bridge connecting Brooklyn with Staten Island. I reminded the children that Verrazano had been a famous Italian explorer. We sat in the convertible, gazing up in wonder at this engineering marvel with its tangible lessons in physics and geometry. Photography was my passion. I owned a collection of cameras and over the years documented everything from changing construction sites to the equally rapid progression of my children's development. If I missed capturing on film the split second when a child blew out the birthday candles, I would relight the candles and ask him or her to start again. That would always evoke the familiar "Oh, come on, Dad. Not again."

I took photographs of everything. It was my way of not missing a moment, of embracing an experience that might otherwise have occurred without my fully appreciating it. In those days, life was spinning so fast that a quick click of the shutter captured a moment's memory that was otherwise lost to time or taken for granted.

$$\circ\ \circ\ \circ\ \circ$$

New test preparation companies were being established, but they were small and posed no threat to Kaplan. In fact, my test preparation business grew so large that by 1967 I was running out of space both in my basement and at the East Seventeenth Street location. So many students were coming to my home basement that my neighbors sought a cease-and-desist order and my attorney went before the zoning board to argue my case. "This case will determine when a school is or is not a school," he told the board in an unequivocal tone. "This is not a school because it's a house. Like a doctor, a lawyer, or a dentist, Mr. Kaplan is a professional who has the right to pursue his career from his home."

He was convincing. The board voted to allow my basement business to continue if I added an emergency exit. That was easy. The hard job was trying to figure out where to put all the students. I rented extra space for classes in local synagogues and meeting halls and began a search for larger rental space.

I had heard a builder was renovating a two-story tenement for offices and stores on East Sixteenth Street, just one block from my East Seventeenth Street center, so I walked over to check on the progress. Once I saw the second-floor space, I told the builder to hold it for me. I rushed lickety-split to call my lawyer and an architect. The lease was signed, and plans were drawn up for a new office and classrooms. I gave the builder my plans and told him I'd give both his children and their children free SAT classes. We shook hands and toasted our mutual success, and three months later the doors swung open to a new Stanley H. Kaplan Educational Center Ltd.

The new space on East Sixteenth Street was an ideal location. I could also design the space to suit my special needs. It had large classrooms, a production area for printing my material and recording my tapes, and office space for researchers, enrollment counselors, secretaries, and Mario, an amiable and beloved custodian. For the first time, I had my own private office. It was just a cubbyhole with a file cabinet, a desk, and two chairs, but I used it for the few students I was still tutoring individually, whom I couldn't bear to give up. One room was filled with reel-to-reel tape players where sixteen students could listen to tapes at any time of day or night.

I hired more office staff—brothers, sisters, mothers, and friends of my employees. My children brought friends from school in the afternoon to file papers and type quickie tests. I hired one person just to keep me on schedule because some days I taught seven classes in a row, dashing from one classroom to another while still putting my head in on other teachers' classes to check their progress. The office pace was so fast and hectic that one receptionist went out to lunch on her first day and never returned.

I was demanding, but I never failed to appreciate my staff's loyalty. I always tried to remember that a smile and a compliment cost nothing and produced great results. I cared about their lives outside the office and asked about their sick mothers, their children's birthday parties, their wedding anniversaries. I rewarded them with bonuses. Because I was so busy with teaching and developing new materials, however, I wasn't always the best business manager and tended to neglect my company responsibilities.

"I have a problem," my bookkeeper announced to me at my office door one day.

"Come in and close the door behind you," I said.

"I'm looking for another job that has benefits," she announced. I paid her like most of my employees—by the hour for part-time work.

"Hm," I answered. For the next hour we discussed a pro rata benefit plan for all employees that I presented to my father-in-law to review. When she left my office, my secretary turned to her and said, "I confess. I heard every word. The intercom was turned on by mistake. Thank you from all of us who work here." Benefits were instituted shortly after.

No staff deserved them more than mine. Everyone handled multiple tasks and possessed an old-fashioned work ethic characteristic of a mom-and-pop business. Some days required more dedication than others. Once I gave my car keys to an aide and asked him to retrieve the payroll checks from my car. He was so nervous about the responsibility that he accidentally dropped the car keys down the elevator shaft on his way to the parking lot. It took hours for the service men to extricate the keys, and no one received a paycheck until the next day. What could we all do but laugh?

My staff took as much pride in their work as I did in their accomplishments, and we worked side by side as a team. One assistant with duties as receptionist, clerk, and bookkeeper refused to accept overtime pay because she insisted she complete her work in a thorough fashion. "I'm staying until it's done right," she said.

My staff gave the customers kid-glove treatment, making sure the students and parents had whatever they needed. I installed a "hot line" from the center to my home phone so I could be reached any time of day. One day a mother told my receptionist that she couldn't pay her son's tuition because she had recently been widowed. My receptionist quickly told her not to worry; something could be arranged. I overheard the conversation on my hot line, immediately called my office, and told my receptionist to waive the tuition. It was the first of many Kaplan scholarships for reduced tuition. I fervently believed that all students should be given the opportunity to learn. At first I offered scholarships to disadvantaged students based on recommendations of teachers and counselors, but as the company grew larger I came to rely on a system similar to that used by colleges to determine financial aid eligibility. Eventually, about 10 percent of my students received scholarships for at least 25 percent of the tuition. Today, through a wide array of local and national programs, Kaplan continues to be a leader in providing educational opportunities for economically disadvantaged students.

Although I possessed a lively entrepreneurial spirit, I lacked many of the necessary entrepreneurial skills. In fact, I often neglected the daily administrative duties of the business because I was so focused on teaching and writing study materials. I relied heavily on my staff to sail a smooth ship and steer the fast-growing business. They handled everything from opening the office each morning to answering the phones, enrolling students, scheduling classes, and keeping detailed accounts of students' progress. The sudden death of Peg Prest in the late 1960s left me with a gap at the executive level, and I placed an ad for an administrator in the *New York Times*. The third person to come for an interview was an energetic woman who had owned a telephone-answering service, and she had wide experience in administration and management. She seemed to be the right person to work with my staff to expand the business, and I made one of my best business moves when I hired Ruth Drucker to be my office manager. "Can you start yesterday?" I asked. We agreed on the next day. As she left, I called to my staff, "No more interviews. I found the perfect one."

Ruth was my troubleshooter, arbiter, idea implementer, pacifier, and eagle-eyed surveyor. I trusted her implicitly. When she made a decision, I supported her. I think we got along so well because we both liked to face challenges; we both liked to work hard; we both believed in our mission. She understood that the purpose of Kaplan was to render much-needed services, and she could see that we were growing by leaps and bounds.

I hired Ruth just in time. Shortly before her arrival, a student who had taken my SAT program showed up to enroll in our new MCAT program. Under normal circumstances this would have been no big deal—it happened all the time. But this student was different. He attended the University of California at Berkeley and would fly to New York to attend our weekly classes! His travel and hotel expenses alone exceeded the cost of the classes. I was flabbergasted, but pleasantly so. Who in his right mind would come from California to take a prep course in Brooklyn?

Soon there were other Berkeley students showing up for MCAT classes who had heard about me from this first long-distance MCAT student. I didn't even advertise in Brooklyn, so I couldn't imagine telling students in San Francisco, "We're having an MCAT course in Brooklyn on Saturdays. Come on over."

But here was an opportunity, and I knew I had a powerful product. There were thousands of medical school applicants clamoring to take the MCAT classes, and we were the specialists. This was the beginning of the MCAT rush on Brooklyn. Students arrived in droves, not just from Berkeley but from colleges in Illinois and Texas too. The demand took me by surprise. There were not just one or two calls, but one or two *hundred* calls. We were ready to produce more materials, beef up the courses, and train more staff to meet the need.

I helped the out-of-town students find inexpensive housing, because almost all stayed ten weeks or longer rather than commute. A widow whose late husband had been a physician welcomed the pre-med students to her big house in Brooklyn and I sent her a steady stream of boarders. Students preparing to arrive for the course called me and jokingly said, "I want to sleep with the widow." She loved to tell this story and years later still asked about the students. I had lots of stories to share with her, because I stayed in touch with many of them after they took the MCAT. They had been part of a significant development of my business. Suddenly the world was beating a path to my doorstep.

6

TAKING MY SHOW ON THE ROAD

It was a sultry day in July 1970 when I phoned Carol Weinbaum, who had worked for me in Brooklyn for twelve years before moving to Philadelphia with her husband. "It's Stanley again," I said. "I'm getting more and more calls from University of Pennsylvania students who want to take an MCAT class in Philadelphia rather than travel to Brooklyn. Makes sense, doesn't it? How about teaching them?"

For years she had rebuffed my requests to start SAT classes in Philadelphia. "SAT classes won't work here," she had insisted. "People here are not like New Yorkers. They aren't as competitive about their kids scoring the highest grade in the class or panicky about which college they attend. SAT prep is a New York thing."

"But this is different," I told her. "I have students coming from all over the country for my MCAT classes. Five students from Philadelphia are already enrolled in classes in Brooklyn, and others want to take classes there." I suggested that she and her husband, who had a Ph.D. in biochemistry, teach classes at their home just one time on a trial basis. My MCAT preparation classes were unique at this time, and students were hungry for my preparation instead of studying on their own. I told Carol I would send all the MCAT study materials, lesson plans, practice tests, and review tapes we used in Brooklyn. Philadelphia would be a clone of Brooklyn. I nudged her with an extra tease: "Maybe you're losing your drive," I said.

She relented. "Okay. Send them on. Let's try one course and see how it goes."

The first class was held in September around Carol's dining room table with a blackboard propped on a chair. I sent copies of my sample tests and study packs. The students began an eight-week review of the basic sciences and verbal and math skills. One Sunday morning, Carol's five-year-old daughter, wearing her pajamas, greeted the students at the front door. "Mom, the children are here," the daughter announced.

During the course, students took Kaplan verisimilar MCATs—very similar to the actual MCAT in length, layout, and types of questions. Because we reused the practice tests, Carol placed a plastic slip over each page and instructed the students to mark the answers with crayons. Then she paid neighborhood children a quarter an hour to wipe the plastic clean with old socks.

The MCAT students must have been pleased, not just by the daughter's casual welcome at the door, but also with the classes, because more University of Pennsylvania students called Carol to enroll. It dawned on Carol that she was signing on for more than she anticipated, but she liked it. It meant she was the first Kaplan administrator to open a center outside Brooklyn. It was a watershed event because now Kaplan had gone national.

The timing couldn't have been better. Enrollment in medical schools boomed in the 1970s. It seemed that every mother in America wanted her son or daughter to become a doctor. There were 40,000 applications annually for only 15,000 medical school slots, meaning that scoring well on the MCAT was crucial for acceptance. I wanted my students to have the opportunity I'd never had to show their full potential by performing their very best on the MCAT. We placed Kaplan flyers around college campuses and bought our first print ads in publications circulated among college students.

The idea of Carol teaching only one course on a trial basis now seemed ridiculous. She held class after class in her dining room and then in her third-floor guest quarters. Finally she rented rooms in a local synagogue and accepted more students, but they still showed up at Carol's home at all times of the day to listen to review tapes. We were producing more study materials than ever before. Every week my staff in Brooklyn delivered practice tests, cassette tapes, and lesson plans by car to Philadelphia. There were no overnight delivery services, and this was the only way for the materials to arrive on time. The students' futures depended on it.

Not everyone in Philadelphia, however, greeted us with open arms. Teachers, counselors, and admissions officers believed the College Board claims about coaching, and they were opposed to anyone who dared to make a profit in education. The campus newspaper at the University of Pennsylvania refused to print our ads because the editor believed our services were unethical. It seemed senseless that the paper accepted ads from Coke but refused ours. The university denied our requests to pin up our posters on campus walls and bulletin boards. Sometimes we posted them on walls at the edge of campus, but they were routinely ripped down. The university refused to rent us rooms, so we taught classes in hotel rooms as close to the campus as possible. Kaplan was definitely persona non grata at the University of Pennsylvania.

Even though the University of Pennsylvania required high test scores in its admissions process, the administration considered Kaplan classes to be outside traditional academic pursuits that did not enhance academic life or the university experience. We responded to this elitist attitude by distributing T-shirts to our students that read, "I UPPED MY SCORES AT STANLEY H. KAPLAN. UP YOURS!"

A month after the first MCAT course was held in Philadelphia, I called my sister, Rosalie, in Washington, D.C., where I also had students waiting to take MCAT classes, and offered the same proposition to make her and her husband instant entrepreneurs.

"Will you do it?" I asked.

"How can one of your first students say no to the best geometry teacher I ever had?" she quipped.

Her husband, Gene, was a Ph.D. biochemist for the government, and I knew they would make a good team. My greatest fear about classes being taught outside Brooklyn was that I would lose control over the quality and consistency of the classes. So to ensure uniformity, I chose people like Gene and Rosalie whom I could trust to follow my guidelines. That was one of the many advantages of hiring family members. No screening or evaluations were needed. I knew from the very beginning whom I could rely on to carry out the Kaplan program. And they invested as much creativity, time, and energy in the program as I did.

Gene and Rosalie spread the word around Johns Hopkins University in nearby Baltimore that they were offering MCAT classes at nearby hotels. The first class attracted 150 students, and most were delighted that they didn't have to travel to New York for a Kaplan class.

I was ready to take my show on the road. The Philadelphia center had four hundred students in its first year, and I realized that for every student who came to Brooklyn from a distant city, there were thousands who would enroll if I opened centers where they lived. For years I had performance and quality on my mind, not growth. But now that performance and quality were assured, I could step on the accelerator. New ideas, new approaches tumbled over one another in a mad dash to be transformed into expansion—more centers, more skilled managers, more products, and thousands of new students.

I offered classes in many cities, including Los Angeles, Chicago, and Miami. It didn't matter where I went; eager students in every city clamored to enroll in a Kaplan course. Even as the number of students taking the SAT declined in the 1970s, the number of students taking the graduate school admissions tests escalated. Students who had taken my SAT classes now returned, wanting help to prepare for an endless list of graduate and professional school entrance tests: GRE, LSAT, MCAT, and GMAT. I welcomed them just as I had the first student who had asked me to help her prepare for the SAT. We taught classes for every test except a pregnancy test. I stared at our national map covered with pushpins denoting Kaplan centers and pinched myself in disbelief over the tremendous growth. Success smelled even sweeter because we were achieving both our financial and our educational goals.

Sometimes I had trouble managing the growth. Producing top-notch material took time, and my staff, despite their expertise and skills, couldn't always produce the study tools and tests as quickly as I wanted. As a result, I felt that sometimes the quality of the materials was not as good as it could be. I was a perfectionist, and I wanted everyone who worked for me to be a perfectionist too. I worried that we were growing so fast that we wouldn't be able to meet all the students' needs or give them the best teachers, the best facilities, the best study materials. It was good to see enrollment increase 100 and 200 percent a year, but I felt a constant strain to keep up with the demand. We were always reacting to some unforeseen crisis. I remember when one of our teachers in Detroit called me the night before her inaugural MCAT class in that city to say she was too ill to teach. My staff and I panicked. We hurriedly recruited one of our best teachers in Brooklyn to take a late-night flight to Detroit so he could be there bright and early the next morning when the 100 students arrived for their first MCAT preparation class. When there was an emergency, everyone pitched in as if they owned the business.

A happy side effect of the national growth was that Kaplan was now known outside New York. In Brooklyn I was accustomed to hearing "You're *the* Stanley H. Kaplan?" But now my name was recognized in Denver and Dallas. It was a heady and unusual experience for me. *Newsday* and *Seventeen* magazine published articles about Kaplan, and U.S. Representative Bertram Podell of New York, while praising my role in education, was shrewd enough to distinguish my preparation program from cram courses. "The dramatic increases in SAT scores effected through the Kaplan Center are not the out-growth of cramming sessions but rather result from unique, pioneering pro-grams which sharpen verbal and mathematical skills," Congressman Podell wrote in the *Congressional Record* of the House of Representatives.

The opening of a new Kaplan center in each city followed a pattern. First I would interview a prospective administrator, usually a relative or friend of someone already working for me. Sometimes I had other families as admin-istrators opening centers for me. The Trussel family, for example, opened centers all over Florida. The parents started Kaplan centers in four cities, and later their son and daughter opened centers in two more cities. Some administrators quit lucrative jobs in other careers to sign on with Kaplan because they had heard about the potential for tremendous growth in their cities from their family or friends who already worked with Kaplan.

My staff and I worked with administrators to select the best teachers for each of our new locations. We looked for enthusiastic, bright teachers who had scored in the top 5 percent of the standardized exam for which they would be preparing students. Good teachers know other good teachers, so I usually hired teachers on the recommendation of others. They seem to run in bunches, and I rarely advertised. I could usually tell from the first intro-duction whether or not someone had the smarts and personality to be a first-rate teacher.

I installed a toll-free telephone line so administrators could call me at any time with questions, complaints, or comments. "If things go wrong, I want to know about it," I told them. "Usually one doesn't check into a hotel and eight weeks later complain about a cockroach you found in your bed the first night."

I hired a specialist to help select and then train the teachers to maintain a consistent level of teaching quality at each center. We hosted teacher meetings, encouraged students to report problems with teachers, and conducted teacher evaluations throughout the sessions. Of course, some teachers were just better than others. At one center, students in one class began wandering down the hall to sit in on another class where the teacher was so much more dynamic. We had to hire another teacher of equal appeal so that we could break up what had become an extraordinarily large class.

Rita offered a steady reminder that despite my desire to oversee everything in the business, I had human limitations and needed to delegate more responsibilities to my capable administrative staff. My top aides began hiring center administrators, teachers, and researchers, although I still signed off on their decisions. We also created a staff for marketing Kaplan services in each city, a totally new venture because we had relied so heavily on word of mouth to generate new business. We started a marketing campaign by hanging Kaplan posters, distributing brochures, and visiting schools to introduce Kaplan to counselors and school administrators. "We'll send experts to answer all your questions" was our pitch. "We'll tell you everything you ever wanted to know about test preparation." We were not overly aggressive, however, and assured them we were not proselytizing our own company.

Ruth Drucker recognized how essential marketing and advertising were to our growth and public image. We needed more exposure than our single neon sign above the flagship Kaplan center in Brooklyn. We needed more than posters on school bulletin boards or tiny newspaper ads in school newspapers. Ever since the inception of my business in 1938, I had avoided advertising. It wasn't the cost; I felt it was unprofessional. But the business world was changing. Other professionals such as doctors and lawyers were now advertising. And my competitors, while still smaller than Kaplan, were advertising too. I selected an advertising agency to design newspaper ads with an owl wearing a mortarboard as my logo. One ad read, "Whooooo's Afraid of the SAT?" My favorite advertising gimmick was a bumper sticker that read, "Kaplan Students Pass with Ease."

Every Sunday we placed an ad in the education section of *The New York Times* because it gave us credibility in the serious academic world. It didn't matter to us how much business it generated; we ran the ads to establish a national image as a credible educational institution and to counter the test makers' propaganda that the coaching industry was a sham. We advertised Kaplan on the radio, bought billboard space, and placed ads in local newspapers. We even advertised on bowling alley score sheets.

The ads focused on what students wanted: improved scores. "Thousands have earned increases of a hundred points or more in their scores," one ad stated. But we made no surefire guarantees. When students asked me how much they would improve their scores, I answered, "I don't know. That depends on you." Very few scores went down, some stayed the same, but most went up. I stressed that the most important gains were gains in knowledge, not just in numbers.

We weren't the only company touting success in our advertisements. In fact, the main impetus behind our decision to advertise was that our competitors—including Sexton, Evergreen, LSAT Review Course of Massachusetts, Amity LSAT, and LSAT Method—were boasting improved scores in their advertisements. There was a full-fledged score-claim game under way. Some companies were truthful when they advertised score improvements. But other unethical companies made outrageous claims of large score gains that appeared to be picked out of a hat while low gains were tossed into a wastebasket. There was no way for consumers to differentiate between fact and fiction. The fly-by-night companies usually didn't last long, but they made the whole test preparation industry look bad. I never liked playing the score-claim game, but I felt that dishonest claims by other companies worked against my efforts to bring credibility to the test preparation industry. So we stepped up our advertising. I wanted everyone to know that Kaplan students scored test points the old-fashioned way: they earned them.

We had competitors, but they controlled only a small share of the market. I was surprised by how few copycat competitors I found in the cities where Kaplan opened centers. It seemed odd to me that no one in Chicago opened a full-service center like mine and advertised, "Why have a teacher from Brooklyn when you can have one right here in Chicago?" Maybe it was because the folks who were preparing students for tests were part-time individual tutors or tiny tutoring companies that didn't have the resources of permanent, fully staffed centers like mine. And they lacked one of the most important elements of my success: a curriculum with custom-designed teaching materials, supplementary homework guides, practice tests, and review tapes.

New York remained the nexus of Kaplan and was the fastest-growing center. Oftentimes our crystal ball couldn't predict the volume of new students in New York. Preregistration was recommended but not required, so we were never sure how many students would show up at the opening sessions. One Saturday morning my teachers and staff stood ready to greet fifty students at a hotel near La Guardia Airport. To their astonishment, two hundred students showed up. "What?" I said when they abruptly called me out of a classroom to report this crowd count. "Send in reinforcements," I barked like a general. "Prepare a hundred and fifty more homework packages and deliver them by car or taxi. I'll hire more teachers for the extra students by next week." There was no way I would disappoint those students or myself by turning away anyone.

I expanded our Brooklyn research and production facilities and opened a separate printing office, where my high school student employees lugged reams of paper and gallons of ink up two flights of stairs. I stocked the printing office with the most modern equipment, including the latest advancement in stencil duplication, which electronically cut a stencil from a typed sheet of paper in six minutes. The same secretaries who sometimes had had to type a single page four times cried, "Hallelujah."

When I finished writing a quickie test, a secretary would dash across the street to our printing office and within an hour return with copies to hand out in class—literally hot off the press. Charles Schumer, now the senior U.S. senator from New York, worked in my printing office while he was in high school. I should have known then that he would aspire to high office because he would read the material as it came off the copy machine to check to see whether I had made any mistakes. He studied while he worked. His SAT scores were close to a perfect 1600.

After the materials were printed and boxed, they were shipped to each Kaplan center in the nation. I couldn't produce materials fast enough for students studying for graduate and professional school exams. They were serious, older students who wanted more reading material, more logic games, more math refreshers, more quantitative skills questions.

My materials were unique, and I worried about duplication by competitors. I instructed my staff to closely monitor the distribution and collection of the materials. The only materials allowed outside the classroom were home study guides, for which we charged students a $50 refundable deposit. The tapes were kept under lock and key for students to use only at the centers. Our administrator in Pittsburgh chased after a student when he tried to leave the center with our materials.

Although the materials were copyrighted, I heard rumors that illegal copies of my home study notes and accompanying tapes for medical school exams were for sale in a bookstore in Guadalajara, Mexico. I sent our Texas administrators, Ron and Barbara Blumenthal, to check it out. They found copies of my homework guides for sale for $60, but they were barely legible and included no tapes. So much for my concerns about piracy! With the myriad test preparation books, tapes, and CD-ROMs available today, it sounds as if I was too protective. But at the time, mine was among only a few organizations creating these materials, and they allowed me to retain my niche in the increasingly competitive business. I was going to protect this asset.

○○○○

Teaching was my love, but the demands of the business of teaching increased. Even with support from my staff, I was still trying to do everything—write new materials, teach, train teachers, and open new centers. When I started calling center administrators across the nation at midnight because it was the only free time I had to talk over new ideas, I knew something had to give. Reluctantly, I stopped teaching in 1973, but I continued to train others in the Kaplan style.

With centers opening all over the nation, it was not always possible for me to directly hire or train every teacher. But I wanted continuity in the Kaplan methods of teaching, so I recorded my lessons for training teachers. "Hi to all of you out there. This is Mr. Kaplan, more formally known as Stanley H. Kaplan, talking to you from New York," I said on the tape. "I'll be speaking to you by phone, but the purpose of this tape is so you can listen, take notes, listen again if you want to, and we can have a more effective means of communication." Then I listed teaching tips: listen to the tapes the students would be using, put some excitement into the lessons, get to know your students, teach the subjects and not just the answers, push students but do so gently and pleasantly. It never hurt to overstate the obvious.

Luckily, I had Kaplan clones. My daughter Susan started working part-time in the Boston office in 1974 after she graduated with a master's degree in social work from Boston University. Susan realized how exciting the test preparation business could be and asked if she could join the burgeoning industry I had founded. I gladly welcomed her because she brought organizational skills and a caring attitude. And she was family!

I also needed as much help as I could get in Boston. Like Philadelphia, it was a bustling college town with a high density of students wanting preparation classes for graduate school admissions tests. And many of the Boston students were from the New York area, so they knew about Kaplan. We were growing fast there, and there was lots of opportunity for expansion in the outlying suburbs.

In a year, Susan was heading the Boston office. She had a lifetime of experience, and she was a natural administrator who understood the first rule of a service business: the customer is always right. She went to extremes to deliver Kaplan to the students, even holding MCAT classes in a beer-doused fraternity house at Amherst on Sunday mornings. She had a talent for hiring and promoting competent staff to create a unified team. My daughter Nancy joined forces with her sister after graduating with a master's degree in guidance counseling from Lesley College in Cambridge. Each had her own strength, and they complemented each other. Susan oversaw postgraduate test preparation, while Nancy handled SAT and PSAT preparation. Nancy, who had taught Spanish at Weyland High School near Boston, was a wonderful teacher who worked well with teenagers. Susan was an efficient administrator who made sure everything ran smoothly. The first student to take an SAT course in Boston returned four years later to take an MCAT course, so he studied under both Susan and Nancy.

As with any siblings, there were stressful moments in their efforts to deliver the best. But they were always able to iron out their differences without my interference. Assertiveness must be a Kaplan trait, because there was no lack of it among my family in the business. That was good, because it translated into steadfast loyalty, dedication, and hard work. But it also displayed itself in a strong clash of confident personalities. When the children were young, we established a rule that we would never talk about the business during lunch or dinner. We needed time as a family away from the business, and it was the one time during the day to separate business and pleasure. We almost always kept true to that rule.

Boston was my favorite center to tour because I could visit my daughters. On one visit I began talking to the taxi driver who drove me to Susan's home. He had come to the United States from Kiev with his brother, who was studying to become a doctor. "He's preparing for his tests at Kaplan," the taxi driver said, not knowing me from Adam. He told me that Kaplan was an important key to his brother's anticipated success in America. How appropriate this conversation was in Boston, where the American struggle for freedom began.

When we arrived at my destination, I got out of the cab and turned to him. "By the way," I said. "I'm Kaplan." He stared in disbelief.

By December 1975, I had opened Kaplan centers in twenty-three cities from coast to coast. While the cost of opening centers was small, the payback was large for both Kaplan and the center administrator. Some years my revenues increased by 30 percent, 50 percent, even doubled. When I opened a new center, I paid the opening costs, overhead, and teachers' salaries. I also sent volumes of materials designed specifically for each course. Centers were not opened as franchises because I wanted complete control over the quality of the courses. Instead, center administrators were independent contractors who earned a 25 percent commission on the center's revenues. It was a profitable opportunity for an enterprising administrator, who needed to invest nothing up front except hard work.

Although I strove for uniformity among the centers, there were marked differences from city to city. For instance, Omaha had a small center serving several hundred students who were just as eager and intent to learn as students in Los Angeles. But the Omaha administrator had different responsibilities from those of his or her counterpart in sprawling L.A. I drove through miles of cornfields to get to the Omaha center. The tempo of life was slower. But our Omaha center and its staff offered a cozy, friendly atmosphere for the students. Centers in large cities had smaller satellite branches in outlying areas, and the administrators couldn't possibly create the same homey climate as in Omaha. But the staff at larger centers had other special talents. Some created their own advertisements geared to their particular customers. The Chicago center staff used brochures and posters that we sent from New York but also created a flyer showing me wearing large glasses and a caption that read, "Stan is a Spectacle."

Adapting tried-and-true methods to regional variations was becoming our forte. As in the past, I relied on tape recorders to meet different needs. A small group of medical students at Temple University in Philadelphia was struggling to pass the three-phase national medical boards administered by the National Board of Medical Examiners. They had taken the MCAT exams to get into medical school and now needed to pass the medical boards in their second year of medical school to graduate and become accepted to residencies and internships. Today the national medical boards are called the U.S. Medical Licensing Exams (USMLE). Word had spread that taking the national medical boards without Kaplan preparation was chancy.

I assembled a staff of medical students and interns in Brooklyn and designed a taped course reviewing all the subjects taught in four years of medical school. Although Kaplan offers live USMLE classes today, we didn't offer live classes then because medical board teachers were difficult to find, the needs of the students varied, and the small classes couldn't cover the costs of voluminous study materials, tapes, and highly paid physician teachers. I sent the tapes and materials to our Philadelphia center for students to study independently. It was the first time I prepared students exclusively with tapes and no live teachers. "Welcome to Kaplan," students heard me say on the tapes. "Remember that if you think I'm talking too quickly, it's really because you're listening too slowly."

My voice on the tapes was as coarse as the sound of car wheels on a gravel road. I was nearly drowned out by background noises of police sirens, chatting employees, and slamming doors. Students listening to the tapes in Philadelphia would burst into laughter when they heard me fitfully quelling the interruptions. "Quiet back there!" I would say with the recorder still running. "I'm trying to record a lesson. Quiet!"

I also sent the students practice tests with answers and explanations. "A word of warning," I admonished. "Don't look at somebody else's answers during a practice test. Don't just look at the answer sheet and copy them without doing the homework. You're only fooling yourself. It's like going to a doctor and bringing someone else's urine samples. Who are you kidding? I'll tell you who—yourself! And you won't be prepared come test day."

There were other medical students who had not been accepted by one of

America's 116 medical schools and had opted to attend "offshore" medical schools in Italy, France, the Philippines, Mexico, Grenada, and the Dominican Republic. But to return home for clinical clerkships and residencies, they were required to pass more difficult national medical boards administered by the Educational Commission for Foreign Medical Graduates (ECFMG). Many headed straight for our Brooklyn center after stepping off the plane.

We also experienced an influx of non-American students who wanted to practice medicine in America. Many were already doctors in their native lands, while others had recently graduated from foreign medical schools. They also were required to pass the national medical boards and a Clinical Skills Assessment (CSA) exam to demonstrate English proficiency. They had special needs because the preparation included remedial English classes, training in medical terminology, and extensive refreshing if they had graduated from medical school years before.

The issue of foreigners coming through the "back door" to practice medicine in America was highly controversial among medical professionals, who questioned the foreigners' qualifications and feared the competition. I met these foreign doctors, however, and I could see they were quality physicians. They simply needed help to prove their potential. Some were refugees from the Soviet Union and Vietnam who were good doctors in their own countries but needed training in American medicine and terminology. Some were more capable than others. But imagine an American passing a medical exam in Russia or Vietnam.

Opposition to them by the American medical community had racial overtones too, which bolstered my decision to help them pass the tests. I received a lot of flak from pre-med advisers and medical associations for helping foreign doctors pass the exams. But it didn't bother me as much as the opposition I had encountered in previous years, because my business was more established and I had more confidence now in my teaching. I was now a heavyweight in test preparation. I was proud of helping people reach their goals, and I knew I was doing the right thing.

It was a wonderful feeling to help someone get his life back on track. I'll never forget a former Romanian doctor who came to see me in my New York office. "I know you're busy," he said, "but I want to tell you how thankful I am. I have taken the ECFMG many times and failed. In Bucharest I was the chief radiologist; here I have been a nurse. I took a Kaplan course and finally passed the test. For the first time in ten years I feel like a man again." Watching students fulfill their potential was my biggest reward.

One summer Rita and I traveled to Japan, where I immediately ruined our vacation with a case of severe stomach cramps. Rita called a physician, who gave me a thorough examination and prescribed some medicine. "No charge," he said. "You probably don't recognize me because I've grown a mustache, but you helped me get into college and medical school. I still remember the corny joke you cracked about the dangers of the tsetse fly: 'Now, don't let this bug you, Melvin.' "

Some Kaplan centers across the country began looking like a mixture of immigration office, religious temple, and Russian bar. Some students in Brooklyn clambered to the rooftop with prayer rugs tucked under their arms while others bathed their feet in the center's bathroom sink. Pairs of shoes lined the front entrance, the aroma of curry filled the classrooms, and we discouraged the Russian students from lugging bottles of vodka to the office kitchen. Once my secretary had to break up a fistfight between a Russian student and a Polish student, and luckily no one was hurt. We were a veritable United Nations, a home away from home, a melting pot of cultures. Students came from the Fiji Islands, Afghanistan, Zambia, Saudi Arabia, and Taiwan. A plastic globe covered with postage stamps—one for each of the 106 countries represented by our students—still sits on my desk as a reminder that our presence is global.

I had the advantage of establishing the right business at the right time in the right place. We had taken advantage of every twist of fate, but we also worked hard to steer our fortune. We had been ambitious and patient and had rolled with the punches. Luckily I rolled well, because things were about to get rougher.

EVENING THE SCORE

My secretary delivered the news at my Brooklyn office. "There's a call on line one from Boston, someone from the Federal Trade Commission," she said nonchalantly.

"The FTC?" I asked. Was I big enough to be called by a regulatory agency of the federal government? "What do they want?"

"I don't know," she said.

I picked up the receiver and spoke to a man with a bureaucratic monotone. He told me that the FTC office in Boston was conducting a preliminary inquiry into whether or not Kaplan had used false advertising and deceptive marketing practices that might violate federal trade laws.

"What?" I was incredulous.

He said his office was looking into my advertisements in Boston that said Kaplan students had improved their SAT scores by an average of 100 points.

"Well, they did improve their scores. That's the gospel truth," I said.

The FTC was only gathering information to decide whether or not a full investigation was warranted, he said, and he asked for my cooperation. "Of course I'll cooperate," I told him. "I'm sure the commission will find my claims rest on solid ground."

I didn't know it at the time, but I later learned that the FTC considered my company a scam that was defrauding students of millions of dollars by falsely claiming to raise their scores on entrance exams. An FTC internal memo written at the time stated, "In light of the increasing competitiveness for a place in colleges and graduate schools, these representations would appeal to all segments of society seeking entrance to institutions of higher learning, and more particularly to graduate schools in the professions. Since these courses sell for $250 and are probably worth closer to $5, almost the entire sales figure for the aptitude courses constitutes consumer injury."

I hung up the phone and wondered what had prompted this inquiry. I called my attorney. I was ready to fight anyone who challenged my teaching philosophy and methods or my score improvement claims.

A few months later, in September 1975, I received a thin envelope from the Boston office of the FTC. I slit open the envelope and read the letter:

Dear Sir: The Boston Regional Office of the Federal Trade Commission has been directed to conduct a formal investigation of the advertising, marketing, and sales practices of Stanley H. Kaplan Educational Center Ltd. It is requested that the following information and materials be made available to the Commission's representatives.

Now we were getting somewhere. The investigation was no longer preliminary, but formal and full-fledged. That meant I had an opportunity to present my case. No matter how hard I had tried to explain my methods and technique over the years, I was still classified with unethical test prep providers. The debate over coaching and its legitimacy had finally come to a head. I welcomed the opportunity to vindicate my claims and prove that coaching worked.

The FTC letter listed a dozen requests for documentation, including total gross annual sales volume, the names of my advertising agencies, lists of our courses with prices and student enrollment, and access to my staff for interviews.

The penultimate request in the letter cut to the heart of the investigation. We were required to substantiate our claims of score improvements with statistical evidence to prove that our courses were beneficial to the students. That would be easy. For years, I had kept students' scores on their diagnostic tests and the PSAT and the actual test scores students had sent me after taking my course.

I would make available all the information I had on every segment of my business. But there was one last request that I could not honor. The FTC wanted the names and addresses of all my students since 1972, their correspondence about customer satisfaction, and Kaplan surveys they had completed. This request went too far because it invaded the privacy of the most cherished aspect of my business: my students. It was one matter to open up all my business books, another to reveal information about my students.

My attorney and I drafted a letter of response. It said that my center had been in business for almost forty years and that we helped students reach their maximum potential.

"We can't claim, of course, that we can help everybody," my letter stated, "because some people might already be at their maximum potential. We can't work any miracles. Perhaps the most convincing evidence of the value of our services comes from the recommendations of former students and also from the hundreds and hundreds of letters that we receive expressing their appreciation for what we have done and also thanking us for helping them further their careers."

We emphasized that Kaplan was one of a cadre of test prep companies that offered SAT preparation courses. "We are fully confident that the investigation will find the wheat will be separated from the chaff," my letter stated.

A week later an FTC attorney from Boston arrived in Brooklyn to interview me. I was cooperative but emphatically denied the College Board's claims that the tests were uncoachable. "I can help students score better on these tests," I told the attorney. "In fact, according to the College Board's own definition of the SAT as a test of developed abilities, I *should* be able to help them. We do the development." I presented the argument I had made so many times before: aptitude is a sum of knowledge that students derive from school and life experiences and the ability to use that knowledge. The knowledge and skills needed on the SAT can be taught. No one pops out of the womb knowing, for instance, the Pythagorean theorem. It has to be taught.

The FTC attorney's follow-up question almost knocked me off my seat. "You stated that no one could figure out the Pythagorean theorem on one's own. Didn't Pythagoras do that?" he asked me.

I thought he was joking. Surely he didn't believe that every student, or even a few students, were capable of thinking like Pythagoras. "Obviously, there are geniuses who might do that," I replied. "But I leave that to the mathematical cognoscenti, not the average or even superior student."

He laughed, but I kept driving my point home. The SAT math section required knowledge of fractions, decimals, percentages, and graphs, as well as the right-triangle formula devised by Pythagoras. We teach and refresh those skills, I told him. Coaching doesn't threaten the validity of the test; it makes the student perform better.

"Preparation can help educated students raise scores from four hundred to four hundred fifty or five hundred points, but rarely from four hundred to seven hundred points," I said. "Most people perform below their potential. I can't work magic, but I help them reach their full potential.

"When I say students can improve an average of a hundred points, that means *average*," I explained. "One student might improve two hundred points while another might not improve at all. Therefore, the average improvement of those two students is a hundred points."

After an hour of interrogation, I had the feeling I had gained the attorney's respect and convinced him that my point of view had the credibility of experience. "Most of my students are referred to me," I said, "and I don't rely heavily on advertising to increase enrollment." I explained our teaching approach: our classes were small and the review was intensive and long-range. We were not a cram school where an impossible amount of material was squeezed into an impossibly short amount of time.

I welcomed the investigation (though I felt a little lonely and annoyed as the only company being investigated) because I thought it eventually would separate the Kaplan organization from the fly-by-night operations. I told the FTC that disreputable test prep companies that tainted the whole industry should be investigated. But ours was not one of those companies. We had programs that were educationally sound. We were a solid company with permanent locations open seven days a week for students. We didn't pack up and run out of town the day after the tests were given.

The FTC lawyer asked me if a discrepancy existed between students who could and could not afford my classes. Absolutely not, I replied. I had never intended to create a division between "haves" and "have-nots." In fact, we regularly awarded partial scholarships based on a student's needs.

"There's something important to remember," I told him. "Test preparation companies don't replace mainstream education, they merely supplement it." I reminded him that private schools, colleges, and universities also provided only a limited number of scholarships and that not all of the nation's academically qualified students attended those schools.

He left my office apparently satisfied with the answers. But this was just the beginning. I had given him something to think about more than just advertising practices. Now we were talking about the role of coaching and standardized admissions tests in American education. That was a much bigger bone to chew on. I could see that this investigation might extend beyond the purview of my single business, eventually scrutinizing the entire industry of coaching companies, the College Board, and other test makers.

In one respect, the investigation didn't surprise me. The testing industry—including test makers and test coaches—was unregulated and not monitored, and these enterprises were growing bigger every day. There had been short-lived rumblings in the U.S. Congress and some state legislatures to require test disclosure by the test makers, but no action had been taken. This FTC investigation charted a new path of possible federal oversight, and it appeared as if I was the primary target—and star witness.

Could it be that the FTC was trying to gain some control over the test makers' monopolies by challenging Kaplan's results? If the claims of Kaplan were sustained, then the College Board's claims that preparation was ineffective wouldn't hold water. If Kaplan was right, the College Board and the ETS were wrong. It couldn't cut both ways.

By the 1970s, the sheer size and influence of both Kaplan and the College Board justified a growing number of questions from not only the government, but also the public and the media. The ETS became more puissant every time another student registered to take one of its tests. Since its inception, the ETS had swelled from two hundred employees and a $2 million gross annual income to two thousand employees and a $50 million gross annual income in 1973. It had moved from downtown Princeton, New Jersey, to a sprawling four-hundred-acre "campus" in nearby Lawrence Township with a convention site, golf course, and hotel. It was so big it had its own zip code. It was the largest private testing institution in the nation, and its parent College Board was made up of 2,300 member colleges and universities. As long as testing thrived, so did the College Board and ETS. And testing was thriving. In 1950, only 75,000 students took the SAT. Twenty-five years later, 750,000 students took the SAT and another 3 million students took other ETS tests. More students than ever were taking test preparation classes, pushing the controversy of coaching to the forefront of national debate.

I believed in the SAT. I should have been one of the ETS's greatest allies. Instead, I found myself a thorn in the ETS's side because I threatened the value of its products. I was its nemesis, and the more students sought coaching, the deeper the College Board dug in its heels. In 1968, it reissued its "green book" with its message that coaching was subversive to the quality of education. The College Board said that coaching for the SAT had caused education to become "unwillingly corrupted in some schools to gain ends which we believe to be not only unworthy but, ironically, unattainable."

The ETS also commissioned in-house researchers to study more thoroughly the effects of coaching on its tests, especially when it wanted to introduce a new type of SAT quantitative comparison math question. In 1972, two ETS researchers, Frank Evans and Lewis Pike, were assigned to test the coachability of the new questions and the math section of the SAT as a whole. The study caused some concern within the ETS, and one executive wrote a memo asking, "What are we going to do if these guys get results?" Another executive told him not to worry: coaching doesn't work. The study results were not what the ETS wanted to hear. The Pike study concluded that the math section was susceptible to coaching and that students could improve their scores with even short-term instruction. Therefore, the validity of the test was questionable, the report concluded. Some researchers at the ETS said the study was sound, and the ETS recommended that the test not include the new quantitative comparison math questions. But others at the ETS were outraged with Pike, and though the study was published, it was never widely circulated. Pike's report discouraged the ETS from conducting more studies at that time that might question the SAT's credibility. Pike was fired, but the ETS and the College Board claimed that his departure was unrelated to his studies but rather was part of a downsizing.

The report came at an especially bad time for the ETS despite its tremendous growth. The number of students taking the SAT was declining from its peak in the 1960s, thereby reducing the amount of money flowing into the ETS. The public was demanding more oversight of and accountability for the testing process. The news media were questioning the authority and monopoly status of the ETS. Consumer activists were asking: Were the tests that could make or break an academic career valid? How did students know the ETS had not made mistakes when grading the tests or when sending more than a million scores to colleges each year? One cartoon drawn by an activist group depicted a lone warrior cracking a whip in battle against a three-headed dragon guarding a castle gate labeled "College of Your Choice, Medical School and Law School." One head of the dragon was labeled "LSAT," another "SAT," and the third "MCAT."

One young maverick leading the charge against the ETS was Ralph Nader, a rising crusader who was challenging corporate goliaths. Flushed with a victory over General Motors that required the giant automaker to build safer cars, he turned his attention to the ETS and canvassed college campuses to denounce standardized testing. He believed the tests were biased against minorities and women, and he saw no redeeming qualities in instruments that failed to measure wisdom, experience, idealism, imagination, stamina, creativity, judgment, and determination. The reliance on standardized tests, he said, was leading us to standardized thinking and standardized curricula. He asked the FTC to investigate the ETS for creating a monopoly that fleeced students, but the FTC replied that the ETS couldn't be guilty of making a profit since it was a nonprofit organization. But the public debate over test accountability, bias, validity, and coaching had reached such a crescendo that the FTC reacted by initiating its investigation of my company.

In March 1976, FTC investigators interviewed ETS representatives who said their statements about coaching were based on studies that had shown that coaching schools had no significant impact on test performance. ETS officials told the FTC that they believed that "not only were coaching schools a waste of time, but they served as a breeding ground for cheating on their exams."

By late 1976, the FTC reached a preliminary conclusion: it needed more information. Kaplan was the nation's largest test preparation company, with almost $8 million in annual sales. But lots of small tutoring enterprises had cropped up across the nation. The FTC estimated that fifty thousand students were spending $10 million a year on coaching, and it wanted to expand its investigation nationally to include more coaching companies.

Kaplan was still the focus of the investigation, but now we were part of an industrywide inquiry. Misery loves company. The FTC expanded its investigation to twenty-two coaching companies in the four cities where I had my largest centers: Boston, Chicago, Los Angeles, and New York. The investigation dragged on and demanded my constant attention. For two years I fought FTC subpoenas to protect the privacy of my students. It cost a lot of almighty bucks, but ultimately I received assurances of confidentiality and submitted the requested information.

Throughout the investigation, Kaplan continued to move forward, and so did the Kaplan family. Rita and I sold our Bedford Avenue home and moved to a co-op on the East Side of Manhattan. The basement center was now a relic of the past. We missed the green lawns and flowers of Bedford Avenue of course, but we had an East River view, and getting to the theater and the opera was now a breeze. It also put me closer to the core of Kaplan operations.

Kaplan had opened two centers in Manhattan, one on Lexington Avenue and another on Madison Avenue, but we soon outgrew both of them and were renting extra classrooms all over town. "Wake up and smell the coffee, Mr. K.!" Ruth said one day. We both knew we were growing too fast to keep renting. We would have to buy—a new word in my vocabulary. But the timing was perfect. New York City was in the midst of a major fiscal crisis, and real estate prices had plummeted. On a plane to New York from Los Angeles, I struck up a conversation with a gentleman sitting next to me, and one bit of conversation led to another. "Did you say you're a real estate agent?" I asked him. "What a coincidence, a stroke of fate. I need a building in Midtown, preferably on the East Side."

"Do I have a building for you!" he responded. And he did. It was the former Grand Street Boys' Club at 131 West Fifty-sixth Street, between Sixth and Seventh Avenues. The club had relocated uptown, leaving this handsome six-story, red brick building vacant. I preferred the East Side, but Ruth seized the option and negotiated a good price. She called me the day before I was leaving on a two-week vacation to China to tell me we should close on the deal before I left town.

"I'll think about it on the trip and make a decision when I return," I told her. Ruth said, "Sign the purchase agreement before you leave. We need to act now. I think the real estate market is about to heat up. Don't chance it, Stanley." And I didn't.

It was a bold move for me, and we closed the deal before I left town. But I didn't know how right she was until I returned from China to learn that one of the biggest real estate moguls in New York had made a much larger offer on the building two days after we had signed. Again, it was another inexplicable turn of fate. That was the story of my life—unforeseen and unexplainable circumstances directing my destiny. Meeting Rita, starting a test preparation business just before a historic upswing in testing, meeting the realtor on the plane, buying this building just in the nick of time—all these coincidences had come to me as gifts of opportunity. Luckily I wasn't timid about recognizing them as fortune and seizing the moment.

When we first visited the building under our new ownership, it looked as if the last person to leave had forgotten to turn out the lights. China and towels, all emblazoned with the Grand Street Boys' Club insignia, were still stocked in cabinets. Photographs of club members hung on the walls, and overstuffed armchairs beckoned weary visitors. We held a giant auction to sell off the contents, spent $1 million to renovate the spectacular structure, and transformed the interior into classrooms and office space. I doubled my New York staff to 150 people, and the building became the nerve center of our rapidly expanding enterprise. Within one year we paid off the mortgage. Within two years the building was overcrowded. This time, I chose to rent rooms in hotels all over Manhattan rather than buy more real estate because much of our enrollment was seasonal and we needed more space only on weekends. Today the Fifty-sixth Street building houses Kaplan International Center, a modern, highly equipped space that serves students from around the world.

○○○○

A by-product of our extraordinary growth and national name recognition was greater acceptance by the academic community. After years of being barred from schools and college campuses, we were finally beginning to forge relationships with college and high school counselors and administrators. It couldn't have happened without dogged and persistent Kaplan ambassadors, however. Ruth Sutton, the administrator of the Pittsburgh center, introduced herself to college counselors and treated them to dinner to explain the Kaplan program. Once her foot was in the door, Kaplan was an easy sell. By 1976, she was holding Kaplan LSAT and MCAT classes on the campuses of Duquesne and Penn State. The University of Pittsburgh provided Kaplan classrooms at no charge—a first! Some schools, such as St. Vincent's College, provided Ruth with a dormitory room for the night during inclement weather. We were becoming part of the academic infrastructure of colleges nationally. A student introduced me before a speech in Boston by saying, "All you have to do is find anyone on campus who is pre-med, pre-dental, or pre-law, and that person will have studied at Kaplan."

We strove to earn the respect of the academic community by attending all the major conventions of high school counselors, school principals, and college advisers for medical, law, dental, and nursing schools. Friendly counselors within an organization would tell my director of research, Fred Danzig, the time and place of conferences, and sometimes he would show up without even registering. The Midwest Association of Pre-law Advisors even began to allow Kaplan representatives to speak at its conferences. Other associations, especially those related to law schools, were slowly beginning to sit up and take notice because we were hard to ignore—more students were taking an LSAT Kaplan course in one year than were being admitted to law school.

As growing numbers of college administrators and advisers realized the importance of test preparation, they began to rely on us for our expertise and refer students to us. They realized that we knew almost as much as the test makers because we spent so much time studying test-taking techniques and test design. In fact, the test preparation industry indirectly contributed to test design as test makers devised new ways to make the test less coachable. Test makers changed the LSAT several times to make it less vulnerable to tricks. We supported these changes, because they produced a better test. Our students never relied exclusively on tricks anyway.

We were usually one step ahead of the test designers, further enhancing Kaplan's reputation as a leader in test preparation. In 1976, the AAMC was scheduled to administer its first "new" MCAT—a test twice as long as the old MCAT, with more difficult and expanded subject matter. Word on the street was that this new MCAT would be uncoachable. It turned out to be the opposite. As soon as the test makers issued promotional material about the test along with sample questions, our research staff began to create a new preparation course. Shortly before the new MCAT was to be given, the AAMC discovered problems with the test and delayed release. Suddenly we found ourselves with a preparation course for a new test that wouldn't make its debut for another year. That gave us a jump start in preparing students and more time to fine-tune our MCAT course. Our actions didn't curry favor with the AAMC, but we were regarded as the experts in MCAT preparation by the vast majority of pre-med students.

$$\bigcirc\bigcirc\bigcirc\bigcirc$$

I was fortunate to have all my children working with me in the business. My daughters were creating some minor earthquakes in Boston. Nancy offered SAT classes in the Boston area and also started small classes for children from kindergarten to sixth grade to review basic reading and math skills. Under Susan's leadership, the Boston center grew to be one of the largest centers outside New York.

My son, Paul, was perhaps the most popular teacher in our Manhattan center—not because he inherited any special secrets from his dad but because he wasn't much older than the students and he naturally bonded with them. He reached out to them, identified their difficulties, and encouraged them to ask questions. His patience was sprinkled with humor, and he was an animated, inspiring teacher. Like many of our teachers, he was interested in the theater and hammed his way to success.

"Spend no more than forty seconds on each problem. That doesn't leave you much time for long multiplication, so never, never, never upon the penalty of death do any arithmetic calculations unless absolutely necessary," he reminded students while punching the air with his finger for added emphasis. "Don't go for the answers only. We don't want you to become NMRs. You know what that is? Nonthinking Mechanical Robots! We want you to be thinkers."

Paul and my niece Rochelle formed a nice tag team—Paul taught math and Rochelle taught verbal. I had no doubts about Rochelle's work experience; her first job for me, in 1965, had been stuffing envelopes with her twin brother, Ronnie, for fifty cents an hour. The Kaplan centers were filled with Kaplans of all ages. The business was our life, and our life was the business. Sometimes there was too much business and not enough family, and Rita would insist that everyone pause in their work long enough to gather at the dinner table.

Some staff members thought our upper echelon of family members was too tight-knit, especially when a Kaplan was promoted over someone of equal dedication and ability. I tried to be sensitive to this, and my daughters went out of their way to give employees extra opportunities to rise through the ranks. Family influence never took precedence over competence. If a Kaplan didn't pull his weight, I never hesitated to move him or her to another position. Too many parents and students were relying on me for the best staff and service. If a family member was qualified and enthusiastic, I put him or her to work.

Paul loved to teach, and he was good at it. But he wanted to learn more about how the business worked. I think he also wanted to prove to me that he was the best he could be because he was part of this very academically competitive family. After he graduated from the Wharton School of the University of Pennsylvania, in 1977, he continued to teach, but I also appointed him comptroller to oversee the financial operations of the national centers. He was a tough manager, assigning strict, yet reasonable, budgets to each center. Some administrators complained if Paul tightened the belt and they missed their budget mark. I stood behind him and told them he was doing his job. But I also told Paul privately to ease up a bit. I knew he was young and still learning the business, but Rita and I had to be firm with him. As we opened more centers, Paul reluctantly gave up teaching to concentrate on center financial operations.

The Kaplan name was becoming as generic as "Xerox" or "Kleenex" without all the X's. Our centers outside New York were burgeoning. We opened a center in San Juan, Puerto Rico, in 1976, our first outside the United States and Canada. A year later we had opened centers in sixteen more cities, including Toronto, Canada, and by 1978 had opened centers in twenty-two additional cities.

Almost all the centers first began in the home of an administrator, who converted a den or bedroom into an office and held classes around the dining room table. Ruth Sutton held MCAT and LSAT classes at her Pittsburgh home and stored study materials and tapes in an adjoining bathroom. Often

U.S. Senator John Heinz of Pennsylvania would talk with Ruth around the dining room table while his son was being prepared for the SAT in an upstairs room. Josh Levenson used the dining room table of his apartment in Madison, Wisconsin, to teach classes for the MCAT and national medical boards. Some students traveled up to eight hours by car from all over Wisconsin, Minnesota, and Canada to attend Josh's classes.

Josh was a perfect example of the kind of administrator and entrepreneur we wanted in our company. He was only twenty-four years old, and he had an innovative, entrepreneurial spirit. And the circumstances in which we discovered and hired him were typical of how we hired a lot of our administrators. Josh went to a wedding in New Jersey one weekend, only to find himself seated next to the groom's mother, who worked for me. When she heard he promoted jazz concerts at a coffeehouse, she said, "You sound like an innovative type. You should work for Kaplan. You're just the kind of young man that company is looking for." Josh interviewed for the job with Sheldon Smith, our Midwest Division director from Chicago, and was impressed that Sheldon drove a sports car with a telephone, which in 1976 was high-tech. Sheldon was mutually impressed that everyone in Madison seemed to know and greet Josh. Soon after, Josh opened the Madison center in his apartment and installed the Kaplan organization's first telephone-answering machine, another high-tech device for the times.

Once word was out that Kaplan was in a city, business grew so rapidly that within a year administrators had to rent space in shopping centers and office buildings. Josh opened two other centers in nearby Milwaukee and Minneapolis but encountered licensing problems with the State of Minnesota. Did that daunt him? Of course not. His creative talents paid off. He moved the Minneapolis center just across the St. Croix River into Wisconsin until Minnesota approved the license. Hundreds of students crossed the river.

Today, Josh is an executive running one of Kaplan's newest businesses. It is gratifying for me to see that Kaplan has many innovative and committed employees like Josh who helped develop the business and continue to play important roles as VIPs in the company.

With new centers opening every month, I spent weeks at a time flying around the country to visit them. I was interested in personally meeting each administrator, teacher, and student. My company wasn't just a business—it was all about people and meeting students' needs. I wanted each student to feel as if he or she were the most important person in the classroom. I also wanted my employees to know how much I appreciated it when they made students feel that way.

The constant travel was exhausting, but I loved it. Back then, planes ran on time, airline food was better, and flight attendants smiled. And I enjoyed meeting new people on the plane. When fellow travelers asked me about my profession, I'd talk for twenty minutes about test preparation. I also learned a lot about education and tests from their experiences. Once a man sitting next to me told me a story that reinforced my most basic belief in the value of a teacher who is positive and encouraging. He said a third-grade teacher told his daughter, "You're stupid. You'll never learn math." And that's what happened. The daughter never learned math. No teacher should ever tell children they are incapable of reaching a goal. I made sure that Kaplan employees realized they had a deep responsibility to our students to be positive at all times. There's already too much tension involved with testing, and our teachers strove to be as pleasant and encouraging as possible.

I loved the hectic pace of visiting Kaplan centers. As soon as I arrived in a new city, I checked in with my staff back at the main office, because I wanted to be available when the daily crisis occurred. There was always at least one a day. I loved to be busy—not nonsense busy but busy doing something exciting and empowering. When a new Kaplan center opened, I was there to hear the buzz around town and answer questions from the local media. The welcome was tremendous, because students and parents were pleased that New York wasn't the only place to have Kaplan test preparation.

My job was to spread the Kaplan message through the media. If I received a request to appear on television in Salt Lake City, I would call my centers in San Francisco, Los Angeles, and San Diego and tell them, "I'll be in your neck of the woods in two weeks. Maybe you could arrange for TV, radio, or press interviews. Coaching is a hot topic, and I'd like to make it hotter."

The media interview questions ran the gamut from a pleasant morning discussion about a new center to a grilling about the increased emphasis on standardized tests. "How can you help students get better scores on these make-or-break high-pressure tests?" one reporter asked me. "What tips do you offer for a good student who is a poor test taker?"

Answering these questions was second nature for me because I had been teaching students to take tests for more than thirty years. I would repeat my mantra: "Since the 1950s and the 1960s, the name of the game has been to do well on a test and perhaps you'll have a better chance to get into the college or medical school of your choice. These tests are general in nature with nonroutine questions. They require long-term studying over months. The rustier you are, the more study you'll need."

In August 1977, a single event focused more national media attention than ever before on standardized testing and Kaplan. The College Board released new findings that SAT scores had been declining for the last fourteen years, and the nation was questioning what was wrong with American education. The report cited a host of reasons for the decline: more minority, female, economically disadvantaged, and academically inferior students were taking the SAT; students spent more time watching television instead of reading; the family's role in education had declined; and students had poor study habits.

One news reporter interviewed students at Kaplan centers who said that Kaplan courses had helped them improve their scores. The reporter said, "If they do help, then perhaps review courses are the ultimate invalidator of the Scholastic Aptitude Test because if you can study for an aptitude test, then what does that say about your aptitude?"

I was in my office watching the newscast and jumped up. The reporter was essentially calling me a quack for trying to improve aptitude, which he considered to be an innate quality. An idea hit me like a ton of textbooks. "Scholastic Aptitude Test" was a misnomer. Aptitude is defined in the dictionary as a natural or acquired talent or ability. Many people interpreted it to be an inherent quality. The word "aptitude" in the name of the test created confusion over what exactly the SAT tested—innate intellect or acquired knowledge? The SAT was never meant to be an IQ test. The "A" in SAT should stand for "assessment"—Scholastic Assessment Test. I liked the sound of that much better. I decided to promote a name change for the SAT when I made speeches and appearances on television and radio.

A name change would also reflect the beginnings of a change in attitudes. Unbelievably, test makers were starting to soften their position on coaching. In late 1977, I appeared on a Public Broadcasting System radio program with an ETS consultant, Dr. Knowland, who acknowledged that long-term test preparation over one to two years could improve scores. His statement was restrained, and he certainly wasn't endorsing coaching. But it wasn't the outright dismissal of coaching of the past. He admitted that scores could be improved by 15 to 20 points when students took the SAT a second time and that every student should be informed about test-taking strategies and grading. ETS was conceding—if only slightly—that coaching was here to stay. The debate was shifting from whether or not preparation was effective to the degree of effectiveness. Years before I had assumed that arguments against coaching would be short-lived because they were irrational and unsubstantiated. Instead, the disclaimer had been resilient and survived, making it difficult to recognize initially that more changes were looming on the horizon.

When the American Dental Association (ADA) invited me to speak at its annual luncheon, I was ecstatic. It was like being invited into the lion's den with the lion purring. I was as nervous as a student taking the dental admissions exam—at least a student who had not taken Kaplan preparation first. It was the first and only time in my life that I spoke from a prepared text because I wanted to be sure that my message was clearly conveyed.

Hundreds of extra chairs were moved in for my appearance. I stood before a rapt audience who wanted explanations of issues that had divided us for years. I first wanted to clear up confusion about how we got the questions for our practice tests. I denied rumors that we stole questions or paid students to memorize questions. "I could not face you—I could not face myself—if these allegations were true," I told the audience. Then I broached the question of whether coaching is cheating. "Is review unfair?" I asked. "Should a student with a 3.5 GPA be denied entry based on a three-hour exam? No. But a standard measurement is needed. Is it unfair to deprive students of the opportunity to prepare? No student should be deprived of that opportunity because of an inability to pay.

"I didn't create a demand for test preparation," I continued. "The students came to me asking for a DAT study course. I filled a void as an educator and not as a businessman. As long as ambition burns, students will seek every opportunity that helps them to achieve their goals. I don't blame them."

And then I choked up for a moment, unable to continue. I was so convinced of my mission to help students, and finally I was able to plead my case. I composed myself and continued with a final word of thanks. Never before had I made a speech with such conviction. I was amazed and humbled when the audience rose to their feet and applauded. For years I had been ostracized, and this group had been one of my most ardent opponents. Now they accepted my work. Indeed, it was my shining hour.

LET THE SUN SHINE IN

In the fall of 1978, *NBC Nightly News* reported that the FTC report was forthcoming and dedicated a portion of its news segment to the issue of coaching. It featured the growth of Kaplan from one school in 1969 to seventy teaching centers across the nation. My attorney told me the FTC would release its report in a few days, and I was tingling with curiosity and confidence.

The repercussions were greater than I expected. Coaching, the report stated, improved SAT scores, and the average increase could be a much as 100 points. My ads didn't say it; a government report said it. At last I felt vindicated. The preliminary report still needed final FTC approval, but the nation regarded it as a momentous decision that shook the educational establishment.

The investigation had pitted the College Board against the coaching industry and declared us the winner. The conclusions were daunting. The FTC said that because not all students could afford coaching, the tests created barriers to education opportunities guaranteed by the federal General Education Provisions Act. The report also stated that coaching "reveals the lack of reliability and validity of these examinations." Therefore, the report deemed standardized tests to be discriminatory against students who could not afford coaching or students who were dissuaded from coaching because the test makers depreciated its value. Here was a clear message that students should prepare for an upcoming SAT if they scored poorly on the PSAT or on a previous SAT.

The report said that coaching courses varied dramatically, ranging from quick weekend cram courses to long-term training with up to two hundred hours of instruction and study supplements. The report cited "Student A," who had been rejected at seven law schools because she had both a low GPA and a low LSAT score. The report said she had then enrolled in a Kaplan class, scored higher the second time, and been admitted to two law schools. All of us at Kaplan were delighted by the report and its implications. Even though we had heard weeks before that the report would be favorable to the test preparation industry, we'd had no idea it would be this positive. We had a big celebration at our New York office with cake and ice cream. I toasted to our future success with a resounding "Well done!" for the staff.

The release of the report also prompted a new wave of media requests. When I received a call from the *MacNeil-Lehrer Newshour* of the Public Broadcasting System, I jumped at the chance to appear alongside E. Belvin Williams, a vice president at the ETS. Now we could present our divergent points of view to the nation.

"It's called the Scholastic Aptitude Test, or SAT," the reporter said at the opening of the news segment. "Admissions boards say it's the most reliable gauge of a student's ability. But two weeks ago, the Federal Trade Commission shook the bedrock reputation of the test. An FTC report said coaching before the test can improve student scores. That finding contradicts long-time guarantees by the test creator, the ETS."

The reporter turned to Belvin Williams and asked him to defend the College Board's contention about coaching. His response almost shook me off my chair. The College Board had never said coaching wouldn't help, he said; it had only stated that the amount of improvement was insignificant. Then he acknowledged that long-term courses such as Kaplan could improve student performance.

The television interviewer was also startled. "But I recall when I took the SAT that I was specifically told that coaching or studying would not at all affect my score. Why hasn't ETS come out and said that a course such as the one Mr. Kaplan runs would be effective?"

Williams answered reluctantly but honestly. "I think most of the argument has always been around the short-term coaching cramming experience," he said. "Unfortunately, that hasn't been made clear in the public statements that have sometimes come from the ETS and the College Board." Students should be fully informed on how to improve their scores, he said, and he encouraged them to do anything needed to improve them. I knew then that the ETS understood the implications of the FTC report. It was softening its position and acknowledging the effectiveness of coaching, because public sentiment had outpaced its outdated position on coaching.

Meanwhile, the FTC report gained the attention of other government officials. New York State Senator Kenneth P. LaValle, chairman of the state Higher Education Committee, was particularly interested in the FTC report because his committee was in the midst of addressing constituents' concerns over the growing use of standardized tests and the criticism that the tests were biased against minorities, economically disadvantaged students, and women. Ralph Nader's grassroots organization, U.S. Public Interest Research Group, backed up by student activists, had been pushing New York legislators for reforms.

LaValle had also watched the California legislature introduce a new "sunshine" bill, essentially a consumer protection bill, that required test makers to publicly disclose information about the tests—how they were created, how they were scored, and how valid they were in predicting future performance. Students at the University of California had lobbied for the bill after the university had proposed that SAT scores be required for admission. Similar legislative initiatives had failed in Colorado, Florida, Maryland, Ohio, and Texas, but California was close to final passage of its bill.

Senator LaValle wanted New York to enact something similar—a "truth-in-testing" law—because test takers, like other consumers, should know what they were buying. He believed all students should be familiar with the test format before test day, and he wanted a law that would allow students to see their tests after they were graded. The public, he felt, should have access to all research on the validity of the tests, including what the tests were suppose to measure and how to interpret the scores. The statute would apply to virtually all entrance exams to college, law school, medical school, and graduate schools but not licensing exams.

I found myself in a peculiar position about whether to endorse the proposed legislation. I had a lot to gain if the tests were released on a regular basis, because I could use them to improve my teaching. But I was also concerned about how disclosure might affect the reliability of the tests. It was costly to produce new tests because questions had to be accurate predictors of ability. Mass production of tests could threaten their quality. Could the ETS keep producing quality tests for each new test date?

Test disclosure might also have a negative impact on my business, because my custom-designed study materials might lose their value if everyone had copies of the old tests. But then I realized that there was much more to attribute my students' success to than knowledge of a test format. It was my unique teaching methods and the students' hard work that produced success.

After much deliberation, I concluded that the heavy curtains should be pulled back to let the sun shine in. All students should have more information about these tests, and the lines of communication between test makers and test takers should be opened. I remembered how the New York Board of Regents had miscalculated my test scores, and I felt there should be safeguards for students to monitor grading and scores. Every so often a student discovered a flawed question on a test. I saluted the ETS that the errors were few, but students should never be penalized no matter how small the "damage."

And the ETS needed to improve its relationship with students, especially when it was accusing students of cheating if their score increases were large. One Kaplan student was required to retake the SAT because the ETS was suspicious of his 350-point improvement. Guess what? He improved even more. Motivated students who improve their scores should not be punished for their hard work. Another Kaplan student in Chicago improved her score by 600 points and was retested by ETS with a proctor watching her—not exactly an unpressured experience for a seventeen-year-old woman. Her score was 20 points higher on the retest, and she was featured on the ABC television show *20/20*. Of course, not everyone improves by 600 points, but it showed that impressive gains could be made without cheating.

Sometimes a student asked me to write to the ETS to appeal its demand for a retest. In my letters I would explain that the student had shown vast improvement during my courses and therefore charges of cheating were likely unjustified. Often, the student's appeal was accepted. But when it wasn't, he or she was required to take the test again. That placed students in an embarrassing, unwarranted, and stressful situation that could produce a less-than-optimum outcome.

Meanwhile, the FTC in Boston sent its report to the FTC Bureau of Consumer Affairs in Washington, D.C., where it was received with reservations. The Boston office had opened Pandora's box, and the D.C. office inherited a volatile, controversial case. Some FTC staff feared that adopting the Boston report could result in a proliferation of coaching schools operating without regulation or government control. Approving the report might also encourage possible litigation by millions of test takers who believed they had been misled by the ETS. There were also valid questions about Boston's research methodology.

The FTC decided that because the Boston office had used uncontrolled research conditions, a more thorough investigation of Kaplan and a second coaching company was needed. The FTC initiated a second investigation that would last another year. My top aides and I were already battle-weary from the first investigation, but we wanted a final, definitive decision that would put the debate to rest.

I was sitting at breakfast one day in early May 1979 when I opened the *New York Times* and saw an article on the debate over the effectiveness of coaching and the legitimacy of the test preparation industry. It said the FTC final report would be released soon but that it had been delayed because rumors were circulating that the findings were favorable to the coaching business. I would have to sit tight a little longer and remain confident that the FTC would find my teaching methods and results were as effective as I claimed.

Just as my wife and I were packing our bags for the Memorial Day weekend, Senator LaValle introduced his truth-in-testing bill. When we returned from the holiday weekend on Tuesday, the FTC released its final report. In a resounding victory for the test preparation industry, the FTC again concluded that coaching could help raise SAT scores, though it cautioned that the findings were not an endorsement of coaching. The report said the average score increase was 50 points after coaching. That was less than my results or those cited in the Boston report, but it was still a score gain higher than the ETS's claims of 15 to 20 points. The report also credited Kaplan with being the most effective test preparation program in its study.

"I'm pleased but not surprised by the FTC findings," I was quoted as saying in the *New York Times*. "To say you can't improve scores is to say you can't improve students, and I disagree with that."

The report also touched on the larger, more relevant issue of test takers' rights and the College Board's responsibility to fully inform students. The FTC report acknowledged that the College Board's statements on coaching had been somewhat more conciliatory since the late 1960s. But it chided the College Board for its position in the "little green book" that had ignored the possible score gains from coaching and insisted that the College Board revise its statements to students. At the urgings of the FTC, the College Board rewrote its handbooks to include more generous and definitive language about the benefits of coaching. The College Board also agreed to provide more information about coaching in future handbooks. A week after the report's release, newspapers reported that the ETS was considering the possibility that maybe the SAT was not as "coachproof" as it had originally insisted.

Senator LaValle began to hold hearings on the proposed truth-in-testing legislation. Among those at the hearing supporting the bill was Lewis Pike, the former ETS researcher. During the hearing, the bill's cosponsor said he had taken a Kaplan SAT course back in the 1950s and it had given him an advantage over other students. Then he asked other committee members: Shouldn't *all* students have the opportunity to practice with test questions beforehand?

The New York State Capitol became the arena of a full-fledged, heavyweight lobbying match. In one corner were parents, students, and consumer groups, who rallied for the bill. In the opposite corner were the state education commissioner, the College Board and ETS, college administrators, and medical and dental licensing associations that opposed the bill. The College Board, which was then giving tests to 3.2 million people each year, was dead set against releasing any of its tests without a fight. To do so would mean higher costs, and the ETS threatened to raise the price of taking the SAT from $4.75 to $8.75. Opponents said the ETS, with its $94 million budget, could afford full disclosure.

I watched as emotions flared and the debate escalated. One ETS official accepted an invitation to speak at a college and found himself confronted by an auditorium full of obstinate, angry students who wanted answers.

"If the SAT is a very important test to my career, why I can't I see the scored SAT when I'm finished?" one brazen student asked the ETS official.

"So that we will be able to reuse the questions again" was the answer.

"How can I trust you?" the student asked, and the crowd burst into applause.

"Because if you have a question about your test, we at ETS would expect you to write or telephone and ask us to rescore the answer sheet by hand, which we do."

The ETS and the College Board had tried to make some accommodations for fuller disclosure to stave off the mounting public pressure. A year before, in 1978, the College Board for the first time included in its instruction handbook to students a composite sample of an entire SAT, not just sample questions as in the past. I had only a rough idea of what this test looked like in its entirety. Now here I was, actually holding a copy of the SAT in my hands. It is impossible for me to explain the thrill of seeing an example of the entire SAT for the first time after teaching it for more than thirty years. In some ways it was so familiar—the questions were much like the samples included in the handbooks. But I'd had no idea how the questions were grouped or presented. I realized I had not been teaching my students everything they needed to know and, in a way, I had let them down.

There were many "secrets" that I now unraveled. For instance, I'd never known that the questions were arranged in order of difficulty. Now I saw that the questions were easy in the beginning and became progressively more difficult. Knowing that would be a major advantage when teaching students how to make educated guesses. For instance, one question at the end of the sample test was "A train is moving from point A to point B at the average rate of 30 mph. The return trip is the same distance at an average of 40 mph. What's the average rate of round-trip travel?" Most students would choose the answer 35 mph. But 35 mph is too obvious an answer for a difficult question at the end of the math section. Right away, the student should eliminate 35 mph as the answer. The answer, by the way, is 34⅔ mph. The train travels the same distance at 30 mph that it does at 40 mph; therefore it spends more time traveling at the slower rate, so the round trip rate should be slightly closer to 30 mph than 40 mph. Once one grasps this concept, it's always easy to pick the correct answer on a multiple-choice test. Simply pick the answer that's slightly smaller than the average between the two rates.

The publication of the first released composite SAT was an important step in giving students more information about what kind of test they should expect. But the public wanted even more disclosures. Activist groups were demanding that students be able to see their tests and answer sheets after the tests were scored.

By July, the New York State Assembly passed LaValle's bill, but Governor Hugh Carey vacillated over signing it. Lobbying was intense from both sides. The bill's proponents held sway, and Carey signed the bill because he said the tests were "imprecise and open to potential misinterpretation and misuse." For the first time, students would eventually be able to see actual copies of their tests and their answer sheets. The ETS had fought, fought, fought against releasing its old tests, but public demands won in the end.

The backlash to the passage of the bill was immediate. The AAMC refused to go along with the new legislation and pursued protection of its MCATs through the courts. Its resistance was based on the argument that writing two new MCATs a year would be extremely difficult. The AAMC threatened to pull the exam out of New York, which meant that students would have to travel to other states to take the test. But saner heads prevailed. The AAMC was exempted from releasing the MCATs, and this exception is still in place today. Eventually several retired MCATs were released to quell public demand. From the first released test, we discovered that the MCAT questions had more sophisticated twists and turns than we had anticipated, and we changed our preparation materials to mirror the MCAT design.

Others applauded the New York law as a landmark victory for test takers' rights. Editorials supporting similar legislation in other states appeared in the *Washington Post*, the *Boston Globe*, the *Chicago Sun-Times*, and the *New York Times*, and articles about the legislation appeared in *Time* and *Newsweek* magazines.

Jon Haber, a young man working in Washington, D.C., watched the New York proceedings with interest. He was a former UCLA student who had helped write a similar California bill, and he now joined forces with the staff of U.S. Representative Ted Weiss to draft a federal proposal. The federal legislation mirrored the New York bill but required the new disclosures nationwide. Only ten days after Carey signed the New York law, Weiss introduced the Educational Testing Act of 1979 to make the New York truth-in-testing legislation national.

The College Board was feeling the pressure of national attention and again shifted its stance on coaching. That same year, a young television anchorwoman named Jane Pauley featured the testing debate on the NBC *Today* show. Her guests were Terry Herndon, executive director of the National Education Association, which supported truth in testing, and E. Belvin Williams, ETS vice president. She was prepared for a brawl.

"When I was in school, I saw every final exam I took," Jane Pauley said to Williams as an opener. "Why couldn't I see my SATs in 1967?"

"There was a kind of policy position," Williams explained, "but I think the law in New York State is a good one although it creates certain kinds of problems. Students should see their tests after they've taken them."

I was watching the television show from my office. Did he say that students should see their own tests? I couldn't believe my ears. Pauley was blindsided by a completely different answer from what she had anticipated. She had invited these two opposing educators, expecting them to wear boxing gloves. Instead they were sweetly dancing arm in arm to the same beat. She shifted in her seat, turned to Herndon, and asked, "You, um, obviously aren't going to argue with that, are you? That's exactly your position."

Herndon agreed. The NEA had supported the New York law. He hoped the federal bill would pass so students across the nation could see their tests as well.

"Well, now that we have that straightened out," Pauley continued, "what is the dispute here? Do we all agree that standardized testing is healthy and good and, as performed in America, is ideal for determining who should succeed and who should not? For who should get into medical school and law school?"

Both Williams and Herndon laughed over whether or not they agreed on that point (which they didn't). Pauley was smart and persistent, and she steered the debate onto another battleground—the increased reliance on tests.

The message was clear: the College Board was finally acquiescing to the public demands for disclosure. On December 29, 1979, two days before implementation of the New York State legislation, the ETS announced that it endorsed the principles of the legislation and that students everywhere would be able to examine the questions and answers on old copies of some of its admissions tests—the SAT, GRE, GMAT, and LSAT. The policy change meant that the requirements mandated in the New York legislation would take effect nationally without Congress needing to enact a federal law.

I was now part of the public debate and appeared at a college forum in New Jersey with Ralph Nader and John Fremer of the ETS. There was a deluge of rain that evening, but I traveled to the college despite warnings of floods that would have discouraged Noah. I wasn't surprised upon my arrival to find no one in the entrance lobby except two members of my staff. Who in his right mind but Kaplan and my employees would be out in this weather? But then I opened the door to the auditorium, and instead of water, I found floods of people. The overflow crowds were dispatched to an adjacent auditorium to watch our debate on closed-circuit television.

Word had spread that there was going to be a battle royal between proponents of test preparation, consumer advocates, and the test makers. I was eager for battle. I gave my adversaries an "I'm going to enjoy this" look and said to myself, "Round one." Fremer started by defending standardized testing. Then Nader blasted it. I spoke last and offered a middle ground of mediation and solutions.

Fremer said that the ETS was about to release the first copies of old tests but that coaching was not much help for a test that measures a lifetime of learning. He said that reviewing the College Board handbook and sample questions was a viable alternative to expensive coaching schools.

Nader objected to what he called the wildly exaggerated significance of tests in almost every aspect of life. "They even have a test for becoming a member of the clergy," he said. "They have a test for almost everything except an entrance to Heaven." That got the audience laughing. "That was told to me by an ETS official in a rare moment of humor and prompted the question whether there's a test for entry into Hell," Nader continued. The ETS and Kaplan were monopolies, he said, with Kaplan being the IBM of coaching. I was keeping good company.

Then I spoke. I supported the use of tests, although as one criterion for admission. I had reservations about the increasing overdependence on them. Use, yes; abuse, no. Admissions tests should be combined with other criteria. Grades alone were not enough; noncognitive evaluation alone was not enough; tests alone were not enough. Grades, tests, and noncognitive evaluation together were the right combination to judge an applicant. And the testing tail should not wag the academic dog. It was important to understand there are limits to standardized tests in the admissions process.

I believed that standardized tests, when considered along with other factors, were essential. Most colleges and universities believed in the tests too. Why had they used them as an admissions criterion for more than thirty years? If I owned a Packard automobile and it repeatedly broke down, I wouldn't continue to buy that brand. And if admissions tests didn't do the job of predicting student performance year after year, the colleges and universities would stop using them. A professor at Johns Hopkins University School of Medicine unofficially used SAT scores to determine admissions to medical school. He said the SAT was such a powerful academic predictor that it was the only test score he needed.

I had personally witnessed how admissions tests opened doors for underachievers, late bloomers, and minorities. Yes, tests compare people, but so do grades. In our competitive world, standards are inevitable, whether for an opera audition, a sports tryout, or a college application. We are a competitive nation, with mechanisms for choosing the victors. It is easy to blame a test if some students do poorly, but maybe other factors are at fault, such as poor schools and inadequate preparation. Ranking students by test scores can be an arbitrary method, but colleges have to have some system along with grades for identifying students who meet their academic standards.

Test disclosure began slowly in 1980. First the College Board provided students with their answer sheets and a scoring key so they could verify that the test had been graded correctly. I asked the son of a family friend who had just taken the SAT if he would lend me his answer sheet and scoring key after he had digested its contents. As an extra incentive I told him that I would review with him any wrong answers. He said he would be happy to help.

Then the ETS released the entire SAT to students after it was graded. In March 1981, two Florida students discovered a mistake on the newly released PSAT that forced the ETS to raise the scores of 240,000 high school students. It received so much publicity that ten days later the College Board

voted to release copies of all graded admissions tests. At first I had fears
that fewer students would enroll in my classes because released tests would
be available to all. But surprise, surprise. Quite the opposite happened.
When high school students preparing to take the test saw how difficult the
test questions could be, they felt an even greater need to seek help, and our
enrollment increased. Here's an example from a 1979 SAT. The students
had twelve minutes to answer fifteen vocabulary questions. One question
asked students to fill in the blanks. "Hume's portrait of Cromwell is irre-
mediably _____: he says on page one what he _____ in later pages. (A)
suggestive..reveals; (B) impressionistic..imagines; (C) abbreviated..re-
futes; (D) tedious..omits; (E) inconsistent..denies." At first glance, that
question could throw a high school student, or almost anyone, into a panic.
But a test taker who has reviewed vocabulary words and understands the
question format beforehand will not be caught off guard. To answer this
question, the test taker must know not only the meanings of the words, but
how they relate to each other in the context of the sentence. That skill can
be reviewed with a student before he or she takes the test.

The release of the tests also generated much more public attention on
coaching and its benefits. Our centers were flooded with media requests for
interviews, and my administrators and I appeared on even more local and
national radio and television shows to promote Kaplan and coaching.

I used the released SAT to create new problem-solving strategies for my
students. "Not every geometry question on the test includes a diagram, but
this doesn't mean there aren't time-saving techniques which apply," I instructed students. "A little common sense is all it takes to give you a leg up
on this question: Two circles with radii r and $r + 2$ have areas that differ by
8π. What is the radius of the larger circle? (A) 1; (B) 2; (C) 3; (D) 8; (E) 9."
First I told students that this question had appeared in the middle section
of the SAT and therefore had a midlevel difficulty rating. So the easiest,
most obvious answers were probably wrong. And careful reading of the
question would allow them to eliminate choices A and B because the question asks for the radius of the larger circle. Answers A and B are wrong because the smaller circle would have a radius that is negative or zero. That
meant there were three other possible answers and students could eliminate some complicated algebra by simply trying the answer choices to see
which fit the conditions of the questions. As it turned out, choice C worked:

If the larger circle has a radius of 3, the smaller circle must have a radius of 1 and the difference in their areas will be $\pi \times 3^2 - \pi \times 1^2 = 8\pi$. The students had to know about radii and algebra expressions, but it was also important for them to know the easiest route to the correct answer. One student wrote a letter of thanks and said she was recommending my course to other "hopeless" math students like herself. "Whether it was the just the math I learned or the confidence you gave me or the combination of both, I just know it all worked," she wrote.

In 1981, the ETS named a new president, Gregory R. Anrig, the Massachusetts commissioner of education and an ardent proponent of truth-in-testing legislation. It was a progressive move that reflected change within the ETS. Anrig, a jovial fellow, was an ETS outsider and former history teacher who had worked his way up through the ranks of public education. He had supported school desegregation and improved services for handicapped students. He was a team player, but he had no intention of insulating the ETS from the general public. He enjoyed participating in the public debate over testing, and he strongly believed that the SAT should accomplish what it had been designed to do—break down barriers and make college accessible to students of all backgrounds. The ETS was recognizing the unstoppable momentum of public sentiment and the possible benefits of accommodation.

THE KING OF TEST PREP

By 1981, I had opened almost one hundred centers in forty-four states serving fifty thousand students a year. I was the country's King of Test Prep. I had been the first to prepare students for the SAT on a large scale, the first to coach for the MCAT, and the first to expand my services nationwide. I dominated the industry, and Kaplan was being imitated all over the country.

In fact, the FTC report and test disclosure brought on lots of new competition. It was inevitable that my company's revenue growth of 30 percent a year since 1975 could not continue unabated. Prospectors who had steered clear of this taboo industry were now eager to capitalize on the FTC seal of approval and used the released tests to devise their own test preparation courses. Test preparation was becoming mainstream, but that meant that competitors tried overnight to copy the teaching methods I had spent decades developing.

Most of these companies, however, couldn't compete with us on the same scale because we were so large and had come on the scene so early. We had spent lots of money to create quality study materials and hire the best teachers. When a new LSAT was given in the early 1980s, we designed a preparation course of such high quality that it was difficult for competitors to match our services.

For years, the test makers had attacked coaching as ineffective. But now that they had shifted their stance, they ironically became one of my biggest competitors. In a dramatic move, the College Board capitalized on the change and began publishing preparation books with copies of past SAT exams. It was unbelievable but totally logical. Who better could coach students on how to improve SAT scores than its creators? Its first book, called

Welcome to this Center

STANLEY H. KAPLAN

Founder & Director

MR. KAPLAN IS ACTIVELY INVOLVED IN TEACHING,
RESEARCH AND ADMINISTRATION AT OUR
EXECUTIVE OFFICE IN NEW YORK CITY
AND IS PERSONALLY INTERESTED IN THE WELFARE
OF EACH STUDENT.

131 West 56th Street. New York. New York. 10019 – (212) 977–8200

4 SATs, included copies of old SATs as practice material. It was the first in a series followed by *5 SATs*, *6 SATs*, eventually to *10 SATs*. The College Board even included a list of test-taking tips in its student information bulletin that were similar to mine. The College Board understood market demand and a good business venture. It was a bittersweet victory that the College Board was competing with me to prepare students for a test it had once deemed uncoachable.

Our most aggressive competitor, however, was The Princeton Review, a company that began in 1981 with a different philosophical approach to preparation. I believed in mastering the tests through long-term development of math and verbal skills. My competitor didn't concentrate on teaching math or verbal skills, just on cracking the SAT, which it considered a pesky nuisance in the admissions process. According to The Princeton Review, the SAT was a hurdle to get around, not over.

The pitch was attractive. Many students, who were less intimidated by standardized tests than those in the past, wanted the quick-fix approach to higher scores. Unfortunately, I underestimated the power of the appeal. The Princeton Review's stake in the market grew fast, and it took me by surprise because I had never before encountered significant competition. Even though it had become fashionable to take one, or even two, SAT preparation courses—one in the spring and the other in the fall—our SAT enrollment was growing at a slower rate than in the 1970s. My competition was gaining a foothold in the territory I had founded years before.

The Princeton Review created a new niche by playing up an antitest message and launching an aggressive, irreverent campaign to distinguish itself from Kaplan. It advertised that Kaplan classes were old-fashioned and abstruse and required too much work for too few returns. It called us a bunch of "humorless cheeseballs." It said our classes were too large and our teachers were stodgy retirees who were boring, boring, boring. "Friends don't let friends take Kaplan," the ads stated.

It was good at convincing many students to try to outwit the SAT. But I was good at what I did—giving students a solid mathematical and verbal foundation to master the test. We may have been old-fashioned, but our students learned something and achieved higher scores. I also had strong name recognition and the respect of educators and parents. At times it was difficult not to go head-to-head with the competition, but I was not going to change my tried-and-true methods to sacrifice my reputation as a master teacher who had been producing impressive score gains for four decades.

Another company also tried to achieve in a few years what I had accomplished in thirty. Janet and George Ronkin started a full-service test preparation and college counseling business in the garage of their Florida home and opened a hundred centers nationally within a few years. They hired away some of my top administrators and office staff and were poised to be serious competitors. But the company went bankrupt and closed when it overstated its revenues to entice investors.

The arrival of new competition wasn't all bad. Competition certainly favors the consumer. Competition was also a wake-up call for Kaplan that spurred us to refine and improve our services. Kaplan was grossing $25 million a year, but my four top executives and I realized that we needed to make some changes.

We reduced class sizes and began to offer extra services such as free sessions on getting into college, writing an application, and conducting an entry interview. One of the strongest features of Kaplan was our unwavering personal attention to students, and we did everything necessary to accommodate their needs. We beefed up our teaching methods and study materials to make them more interesting and stimulating for students. The competition could poke fun at the tests, but I worked to make taking the tests fun.

We also embarked on an aggressive advertising campaign. We bought ads in every market reinforcing our reputation as a serious educational program with a track record. "Stanley H. Kaplan Educational Centers—*The* test preparation specialists since 1938," one ad stated. "Boot Camp for the Brain," read another. We stayed above the fray and didn't engage in competitive name-calling. We wanted students to know that taking a Kaplan course was like trying to lose weight—you could diet at home by yourself, but it was a lot easier to succeed with guidance, company, and discipline. Studying for a standardized test was the same: it was easier doing it with friends, with the help of a teacher, and with good study guides.

We reached out to our staff across the nation to let them know they were an essential part of the Kaplan organization. I sent a monthly newsletter to all my centers to keep administrators and teachers updated on the latest developments with the company, the competition, and national education trends. I visited as many centers as I could because I wanted to stay in touch with Kaplan employees in the trenches. I wanted to talk with the people on the firing line rather than depend on secondhand reports. I believed that TLC was as infectious as a warm smile.

I didn't want to be an absentee owner. I encouraged my staff to come to me with a gripe. Don't let a problem fester until it's too late, I told them. I wanted them to feel that this was more than a job—it was a career.

We established more satellite centers to deliver Kaplan to the students who lived in outlying areas. It was easy to transport our services. All we needed was rental space, desks, cassette tape recorders, teachers, and study materials. In the Boston area, we enrolled several hundred SAT students in twenty suburban locations, and Boston University chose Kaplan as the test preparation company to teach on its campus at the students' insistence. Every Saturday morning, we taught twenty-five SAT classes at high schools and hotels in the Boston area so students wouldn't have to travel far from their homes or schools. When we offered our first GMAT class in Newton, Massachusetts, 160 students showed up. We hadn't anticipated such a large demand, and the students were sitting in the hallways waiting for chairs and desks. By the following day, we had divided the students into smaller classes and hired more teachers.

Uniformity throughout the centers was the key to maintaining quality. At one point, we were offering forty-five different courses, and students were given a Kaplan card that allowed them to attend classes at any center in the country. We wanted to meet every request for service. When we discovered that fifteen students in Albuquerque were traveling more than four hundred miles to attend classes in our Denver center, we opened a center in Albuquerque within a year. As in the past, we were protective of the copyrighted study materials we disseminated to the centers. At one point, someone at one university acquired our study materials and revised them slightly to sell to students nationally for $100. The students who bought the materials probably wouldn't have taken Kaplan courses anyway, so we weren't losing customers. But it angered us that someone was stealing from us. We threatened to sue the perpetrators, and they discontinued their sales.

There were always hitches along the way. As prodigious as Kaplan had become, we often encountered difficulty getting our centers licensed because test preparation didn't fit government classification as either a business or a vocational school. In some jurisdictions, we asked to be exempted from licensing. If that failed, we made personal appeals to state officials. Sometimes an explanation of our program was enough proof that we were a thriving, respected educational institution. However, Minnesota state officials wanted full access to our teaching materials before issuing a license. We refused to give them our sample tests, but we provided review materials, and forty-five days later we were licensed. In some states, such as California, laws were changed or created to include special provisions for test preparation centers such as Kaplan. We also had all our centers accredited by the Accrediting Council for Continuing Education and Training (ACCET) because we wanted to be considered a credible educational institution.

We added new preparation classes to our long list of courses. One of these was preparation for the National Council Licensure Examination (NCLEX) to license nurses, which required more of our attention and resources than some other preparation courses. These students needed more academic training and review than those in other postgraduate courses. NCLEX preparation was already being offered by our competitors, but we jumped into the market by offering smaller classes with a number of extended sessions. Some competitors had two hundred to three hundred students in a class for a one-week course. Our classes lasted for several weeks and featured live teachers and supplemental videotapes.

The NCLEX was different from other exams because the students weren't given a score; they either passed or failed to be licensed as nurses. Our competition appealed to the students who wanted just enough preparation to pass the test. But we offered students a high-quality course that made them better nurses, not just better test takers. I believed the pass/fail system dumbed down the test and threatened the quality of nursing in America. America is losing out when it refuses to identify the higher achievers by not releasing actual scores.

Not all of our new course offerings were successful. I acquired a speed-reading program, but it didn't take off as I anticipated. It just didn't seem to appeal to students, and it required too much marketing to fill the classes.

We redoubled our efforts to prepare students for graduate and professional school admissions exams. An increasing number of students now wanted more than a bachelor's degree, and the competition to get into medical school in particular was becoming more intense. By 1980, fewer than half of the applicants to U.S. medical schools were admitted. As a result, in 1981 ten thousand American students attended foreign medical schools, and many needed help preparing for exams to allow them to practice in America.

When U.S. troops invaded the tiny island of Grenada in 1982 to overthrow a Marxist regime, hundreds of American students at a medical school on the island were evacuated. About thirty students showed up at my Brooklyn center to enroll in medical board classes because they had time off and wanted to keep their skills sharp. It was unsettling for them to be displaced in the middle of their medical school careers. Many had taken my SAT and MCAT classes, so it was like old home week for them to return to the familiar faces at the Kaplan center. They stayed six months, much longer than the time allotted for medical board preparation classes, but they wanted to continue their medical school education at Kaplan while waiting to return to Grenada.

We continued to provide a haven for an influx of foreign nationals coming to America with the hope of practicing medicine. America was in the midst of a doctor shortage. Although our medical schools were graduating sixteen thousand students a year, the nation needed twenty thousand graduates a year to fill the demands for medical care, and medical schools could not afford to train more students. The arriving foreign students needed visas from the U.S. Immigration and Naturalization Service (INS), so we asked local INS offices to give us the authority to issue the visas at our centers. When a center's request for visa-issuing authority was rejected, we appealed to the regional office, and one of our requests went all the way to the INS commissioner in Washington, D.C. We joked among ourselves that getting licensure for foreign medical students was not only driving the business, it was driving us crazy. It took us about two years to get approval for all our centers. But we were the first non–medical school in the nation to be granted visa-issuing authority. Again, we broke new barriers. Each Kaplan center was staffed with a specialist who oversaw the issuing process and tracked visa expirations. We compiled an office manual of do's and don'ts for issuing visas and hired a former INS hearing officer to oversee our international student operations.

One former Kaplan student from Vietnam scored very high on the national medical boards. Years later I was reading a *National Geographic* magazine and saw his picture in an article about physicians filling the gaps in medical care in poor rural areas of America. The article described how he had started a clinic in the Arkansas delta and hired other doctors to serve the area.

Many foreign students were political refugees from war-torn countries. At one point we had a tide of Syrian students seeking refuge from military service in their homeland. There were also Russians seeking asylum from political oppression, and the New York Association for New Americans paid us a $1,000 tuition fee for each Russian student who took our Test of English as a Foreign Language (TOEFL) classes.

I faced one of my most difficult challenges to meet student needs in 1982, when a businessman in Atlanta called the Kaplan center with an idea. He had attended college on a football scholarship and wanted other athletes to have the same opportunity. But that was becoming a bit more difficult. The National Collegiate Athletic Association (NCAA) initiated a new requirement called Proposition 48 that required student athletes to score at least a total of 700 on the SAT in order to participate in Division I sports. Atlanta had a whole crop of talented high school athletes who could not attend colleges and universities if they didn't score well enough on the SAT. He asked me if I would join him in a program to help these athletes prepare for the SAT. No problem, I replied.

With assistance from the Atlanta school superintendent, I sent a battery of teachers to Atlanta to begin a year-long tutoring program. I don't think I have ever had as difficult a challenge to do so much in such a short amount of time. These students faced major impediments to academic success. They came from impoverished neighborhoods and lacked support from their community or their peers to perform well in school. I didn't expect to accomplish major miracles, but perhaps a few minor ones were possible.

This was not a typical test preparation course. Most of the forty-eight students selected by their coaches and counselors had received grades in the bottom 20th percentile of their class and needed intensive training in basic math and verbal skills. We took a tough-love approach. Both the parents and the students agreed to strict rules. If students didn't attend class, they were dropped. Homework was mandatory. At first the students were intimidated, but as they began to improve, they grew enthusiastic and motivated.

The results exceeded my wildest expectations. All but one student scored over the required 700 threshold. The average SAT score improvement was more than 100 points. But I wasn't interested only in scores. The students were seeing a change in themselves. Instead of being only athletes, they saw themselves as college potential. The success of this program illustrated the need for involvement on the part of the entire community: educators, counselors, coaches, parents, and sponsoring organizations. The program continues today as Kaplan's Good Sports Program.

One student in the program improved his SAT score by 300 points and was accepted to the University of Pennsylvania. He was a conscientious student, and after the program he came to my office and said, "I was cheated."

"What?" I said. "Who cheated you?"

"My high school cheated me because it didn't prepare me to go on to college," he said. "I resent that."

He had every right to be resentful. He had been cheated by a poorly funded school system that had inadequately prepared him to succeed academically or to score well on a standardized test. Unfortunately these students, like too many children in our society, had been deprived of that support. For some, our coaching was the first time they received the encouragement and teaching necessary to succeed academically.

The program was part of my goal of inclusiveness. I wanted Kaplan to be a big tent, nurturing people from different walks of life. I offered more test preparation to low-income high school students in conjunction with programs throughout the country. There was nothing more fulfilling than watching these students these gain the advantage to compete in an academic setting.

I remember one African-American second-year medical student who needed to pass part of the national medical boards to remain in medical school. He had failed the test three times. He pleaded with the dean, asking for one more chance. His grades were good, he just didn't test well. He said he was planning to get extra help at Kaplan. The dean must have been impressed with his dedication and sincerity, because he gave the student another chance. We didn't have medical board review classes where he lived at that time, so he drove four hours round-trip to Brooklyn every day. We kept the office open until 11 P.M. so he could study late before returning home. He was the darling of our entire staff. The custodian swept around him while he listened to tapes and took practice test after practice test. I knew he was catching on because he began to smile more. Test day came, and we anxiously awaited his results.

Six weeks later, my assistant came running into my office. I gave her a why-are-you-bothering-me-now look. "He passed," she said. I rushed to pick up the telephone. "It couldn't have happened to a harder-working student," I told him. He received his M.D. degree, and ten years later he called me. He had a successful practice. We had performed a minor miracle.

Kaplan witnessed other miracles as well. We received a federal government grant to help minority students prepare for entrance to medical school. The pilot program was held at the University of Texas Health Science Research Program. During the summer, forty-four college students from around the state attended Kaplan MCAT classes and worked in hospitals and research centers with mentors. Half of them got into medical school. The program was then expanded to other campuses at the University of California at San Diego and Georgetown University in Washington, D.C.

My experiences in working with underrepresented minority students shaped my attitude about criticisms that the SAT was biased against minorities, women, and low-income students. I realized that the SAT wasn't biased; inferior education in America was biased. We needed better schools, not just better tests. A good education should not be a luxury. It is a necessity. The SAT was a barometer, not an instigator, of educational inequalities. Treat the cause of low-test scores, and the scores will increase. I saw firsthand at my own centers what a difference small classes, higher expectations, and individual attention made in students' academic achievement. If a high school senior didn't read well enough to attend college, that was the fault of underresourced schools or a dysfunctional family that had failed to nurture the child's intellectual capabilities. It was not the fault of the SAT.

My support of standardized tests was not, however, an argument against eliminating inherent prejudices or biases in test questions. I endorsed any changes in the subject matter or wording of test questions that would reduce bias. When I first started SAT preparation classes, a majority of the students were white males. My first student, Elizabeth, was among the few women I tutored for the SAT. By the 1980s, however, my classes were filled with a variety of students including women, African Americans, Hispanics, and Asians. And they weren't all high school or college students. Many were older professionals who wanted to change careers.

Unfortunately, there has always been a disparity in education and in access to test preparation. Those who most need preparation are often the ones with the fewest opportunities. Today students can choose from a plethora of relatively inexpensive preparation books and tapes, and many schools offer free test prep courses. But we still have a long road to travel toward equality in test preparation and education. My company has tried to shrink the divide between the haves and the have-nots. I provided reduced-tuition scholarships, introduced teaching programs for disadvantaged students, and offered courses at a discount for needy school districts. Although I didn't advertise my scholarships, a steady stream of needy students was referred to me through high school and college counselors. One high school counselor in Austin, Texas, was highly critical of my service because she said it catered only to students who could afford the tuition. She called me at my New York office to complain. I was anxious to hear her out, so I flew to Austin to meet her. I told her I offered scholarships to students who were short on money but tall on potential. Over the years she referred hundreds of students to me who were unable to pay.

○○○○

Ruth, with her quintessential talent for making shrewd business moves, never let the door of opportunity shut before she thrust in her foot. She kept an eye on not only our enrollment and our curriculum, but on our infrastructure as well. This was especially true in regard to our Fifty-sixth Street building. The real estate market had improved dramatically since our purchase, and the entire block was undergoing rapid renovation and development. We were sitting on hot property in 1982 when our next-door neighbor came calling. He was a real estate tycoon who wanted to buy our air rights, or the unused space allowed for a building's height under New

York zoning laws. Our building was only six stories, much shorter than the number of stories we were allowed. But our neighbor wanted to build a skyscraper with luxury condominiums and offices that was taller than the seventy stories he was permitted. Under the law, he could buy our unused air rights. His bidding price made me gasp.

"I'll give you a million dollars for your air rights," he told Ruth and me at our first meeting without blinking an eye.

Ruth was unfazed. "No deal," she said blandly.

"You mean you're turning down a *million* dollars?" he asked in an exasperated tone.

"Yes," she said.

"Two million," he retorted.

"Not enough, sir," she said. "We have nothing to lose by not selling. You have everything to lose by not buying."

She drove a hard bargain, and over the next few months he returned with still higher offers.

"Three million, and that's my last offer," he said. We sensed how badly he wanted those air rights because in the end we settled on a $4 million sale price.

Ruth and I later celebrated the sale by trekking to the roof of the building with a bottle of wine. Above us was a clear blue sky over Manhattan. We threw our heads back, and she pointed up and said, "How would you like to sell that air for four million dollars?"

A RENEGADE RISES FROM THE ROUGH

In April 1983, a major event in education dramatically altered standardized testing and test preparation. The U.S. Department of Education's National Commission on Excellence in Education issued a report card on American education that began with five simple, yet startling words: "Our Nation is at risk." This scathing report, appropriately entitled *A Nation at Risk*, detailed a rapidly deteriorating system of public education. It reported that twenty-three million adults and children were functionally illiterate, businesses were being forced to spend millions of dollars to educate workers, average SAT scores were the lowest since the 1950s, and our academic ranking among other industrialized nations was abysmally low.

The reasons for failure covered the spectrum: too much television viewing, too little teaching of basic skills, and too little concern by families about their children's education. Whatever the reasons, the report's recommended solutions were all based on the same remedies: raise expectations and raise standards. And how did the report suggest that problems be assessed and changes be measured? By none other than national standardized tests. It gave a thumbs-up to the nation's growing reliance on hard statistics that educators and public officials could put their arms around and say, "Look, there's the problem" or "See, our children are learning."

The report, which cost $750,000 to produce, was a no-brainer. Of course the nation was at risk. Of course we would inherit problems twenty years down the road if we didn't heed the warnings. Of course we needed to return to the basics, demand the best of our students, and spend money on education. These were issues I had promoted for years.

It was also obvious that standardized testing and test preparation were now unavoidable facts of life. Perhaps no group understood this better than school counselors, because they were the ones who assessed students and guided them to college and graduate schools. They were beginning to realize that we shared a common aspiration: students' success. We helped their students get higher scores, scholarships, and acceptance into the college of their choice. Test preparation, once perceived as a no-no, was now viewed as an asset, and I had to give them credit for being able to change with the times. They also realized test preparation wasn't going away. Enrollment in Kaplan courses to prepare for graduate school admission exams had tripled in the last ten years, and counselors and educators were hearing directly from the students that test preparation had helped them.

The change in attitudes toward test preparation had not transpired overnight. It had been a hard-fought battle. For years I attended conferences where counselors and admissions officials gave me a lukewarm reception or even turned away when I entered a room. But I believed I could open the ears, eyes, and minds of my detractors and eventually woo them into my corner. I relentlessly appeared at all the conferences of advisers and counselors, proudly wearing my name tag that boldly proclaimed: Stanley H. Kaplan. Sometimes I'd see a wink or a smile when people recognized my name. Then I would approach them, extend my hand, and introduce myself. Most were interested in meeting the man behind the name, and we engaged in frank discussions about coaching and the legitimacy of my business. They had already heard my viewpoint in speeches or in television and radio interviews, but they had their own questions. Did I steal questions from the test makers? Was it fair that some students could afford coaching when others could not? I explained our methods of developing questions and study materials and I detailed our programs for disadvantaged youths. Sometimes I was convincing; other times I was not. My goal was to be recognized as a bona fide part of the educational process, and I mustered up every bit of courage to counter their indifference because I was determined to convert them.

I'll never forget how determined I was to win over the pre-med advisers at a meeting in Southern California. When I heard from my staff and students that the advisers had been trashing the Kaplan programs, I boarded a plane to present my point of view. When I arrived, about ten health advisers were gathered outside on benches under a majestic oak tree eating boxed lunches. I approached them and introduced myself. It was a beautiful warm day, but I received a cool reception. They said they thought Kaplan was in test preparation just for the money. What about students who couldn't afford our services? Why were the fees so high? I had the answers. My services cost money, and my fees were not exorbitant. Some students could afford to go to private schools and get a top education, others could not. I threw into the pot every bit of information I had garnered over the years. Arguing back and forth energized me. I tried to eliminate disparities in accessibility to test preparation, I said, but it was impossible for me to make it equal for everyone.

I spent a lot of time talking with these advisers, and as the day wore on, some of them began to mellow. There were more smiles and fewer "humbugs." They could see that I believed in my program and would defend it to the hilt. The art of communicating had triumphed. This was just a small group I had reached, but little by little it all must have added up, because years later this group awarded me special recognition for my services.

I also gained the support of other associations by sponsoring convention breakfasts, lunches, dinners, and lavish dessert parties. We showed up at the same conventions every year, and soon it was like meeting old friends. That's what we were becoming. Some associations allowed test preparation representatives to hand out brochures at their conventions and, for a fee, set up information booths. At first all the test preparation booths were shoved into a corner near the bathrooms, away from the center of attention. But when the association leaders realized that everyone had to pass us to visit the "facilities," they moved us into the main exhibit area and we earned a spot at the center of activity.

At the booths, we handed out canvas bags with the boldly printed words "Stanley H. Kaplan Educational Centers—Test Preparation Is Our Bag." This was a clever marketing device for its time because canvas bags were just becoming popular and it was instant advertising. It was amusing to watch conventioneers place competitors' handouts in my tote bags. One veteran counselor brought the same tote bag to the conventions year after year. He also carried the bag to his office, and when students asked him about us, he would give them a brochure and say, "Kaplan is a good idea. Try it." But not all advisers accepted Kaplan so readily. Many turned the bags inside out to conceal the Kaplan name. That was okay. I felt that eventually they would turn them right side out for the whole world to see.

There were defining moments of recognition. At one convention of the National Association of Advisors for the Health Professions, I attended a mock admissions session. Members of the audience were given transcripts to decide which medical school applicants should be accepted based on a student's GPA, MCAT scores, interests, and recommendations. Then the panel discussed each applicant and announced its decision and reasoning. It was fascinating and scary to hold a student's future in our hands—even though it was hypothetical. One applicant, a young Hispanic woman, made the panel's cut. Her GPA was slightly above average, but her other qualifications were more than acceptable. She had taken the MCAT twice, and her score had risen from the twentieth percentile to the ninetieth percentile. One of the panelists looked right at me and quipped, "Maybe she took a Kaplan course." The audience chuckled.

This was my moment, and I leapt to my feet. "I've heard hair-raising stories about medical school applicants being asked during interviews if they had taken a prep course," I said. "Is the answer 'Yes' a kiss of death? Is the student blackballed? Students have asked me over the years if they should lie when asked about taking a prep course. I always answer them, 'You tell the truth. Never lie. Tell them you needed review. Tell them you've wanted to be a physician since high school and you would do anything to do your best, so you took a course.' "

Then I turned to the panelists and said, "The student raised her MCAT score from a hopeless 'No' to a very strong 'Yes.' All of you accepted her. If you had asked her if she had taken a prep course and she had said yes, would you still have accepted her?"

The replies came like shots and told me what I hoped to hear: they agreed that taking a test preparation course should not be a factor in making an admissions decision. "Yes," the first panelist answered. "Yes," answered the second. "Yes," said the third, followed by a fourth and final "Yes." And I thought to myself, "Yes, yes, yes, yes. Test preparation is now acceptable and even encouraged."

Schools were beginning to invite the representatives of test prep companies to speak about their services. But I didn't relish attending these forums because Kaplan was clearly the market leader and my competitors often made misleading claims of artificially high score improvements. One competitor made claims of LSAT score increases even before it began teaching classes. These forums frequently disintegrated into petty squabbles and name-calling sessions that were demeaning and unprofessional. Every year, I agreed to speak at Boston University, but only under the condition that I appear alone.

Perhaps the most important invitation to speak came in 1983. My secretary was curious to know why I would receive a letter from the College Board, so she opened it and then handed it to me. I couldn't believe my eyes. The College Board, with which I had been at odds for years, was inviting me to be the speaker at its annual meeting in Philadelphia. It was like straitjacket manufacturers asking Houdini to speak at their convention.

For thirty years I had been attacked by the College Board. But the FTC findings and the truth-in-testing legislation had caused the test makers to move closer to my position that test preparation can help students perform to their highest potential on standardized tests. I had had fewer opportunities to mend fences with the College Board than with the ETS because the College Board represented hundreds of member colleges while ETS represented only the College Board and a few other clients. An invitation from the College Board was like getting a nod from hundreds of college administrators.

And there wasn't much for us to disagree on anymore. The College Board was realizing that Kaplan—the nationally recognized "Test Preparation Specialist"—was entering the circle of legitimacy. The College Board was extending an olive branch that I gladly accepted. For the first time in my career, we were speaking to each other. And lots of educators were listening. I was a renegade rising from the rough.

I remember the deafening silence that descended over the room when I arrived to speak. I thought of the lyrics to a popular song, "O Lord, please don't let me be misunderstood."

"Never, in my wildest dreams, did I ever think I'd be speaking to you here today," I addressed the crowd. "Can one prepare for standardized tests? I think that is becoming a nonissue. The FTC report and independent surveys have proved conclusively that test preparation does improve performance.

"For a student to be familiar with a test does not erode the quality of the test. Some students do very well just reading the introductory information and tips provided by the College Board. But most students want more. Commitment to a regular class schedule and reassurances provided by a skilled, enthusiastic teacher go a long way toward easing test anxiety.

I received tremendous applause. It was music to my ears—a recital of reconciliation. Everyone likes to be recognized for his hard work, and I was no exception.

Later that summer, I picked up *The Wall Street Journal* at the breakfast table. There on the front page was an etched portrait of myself staring right back at me. The headline proclaimed, "IN THE TESTING GAME, STANLEY KAPLAN GETS TOP MARKS AS COACH." I had spent two days with the reporter who interviewed me for the article, but I was surprised about the prominent front-page billing. What a watershed moment for me and the test preparation industry!

The article explained how my business had grown from one classroom in Brooklyn to 121 teaching centers nationwide offering courses for thirty different kinds of tests to eighty thousand students a year. But the crux of the article was a description of my role in the decades-long, acrimonious debate on the validity of test preparation for admissions exams. I was recognized as a leader and innovator in a field that had finally gained acceptance.

But sustaining a good industrywide reputation was an ongoing struggle. There were bad apples that threatened to spoil the reputation of the bunch. For years Kaplan was the only company offering MCAT test prep in Philadelphia until a young University of Pennsylvania graduate founded a company called MultiPrep Inc. It was giving us a run for our money, and we could not understand why it had gained popularity so fast. We soon learned the reason when all hell broke loose during a lunch break on MCAT test day in 1983. Kaplan students called Carol, our administrator in the Philadelphia center. They told her that MultiPrep students were boasting that the MCAT test questions were identical to those they had studied in class. Carol called me with the news. Neither of us could believe our ears. Something had to be done. No one should have had the test questions beforehand. The integrity of the test was threatened. Carol obtained copies of the MultiPrep class materials and sent them to the maker of the test, the Association of American Medical Colleges. The AAMC filed suit against MultiPrep, alleging it had prepared students with copyrighted MCAT tests that had not been released to the public. I saluted the AAMC for its swift and stern reaction.

In 1984, a MultiPrep executive pleaded guilty to two counts of stealing MCAT questions. MultiPrep students were required to retake the test. Tests are too important not to be secure, and cheating on a test robs other applicants of their rightful places.

The test prep industry that I had created forty years before had changed dramatically. There was the constant turnover of new players, new rules, and new playing fields. And now we were on the brink of even bigger changes brought about by technology, the rapid dissemination of information, and continued public demands for even better educational performance.

KNOCK, KNOCK. WHO'S THERE? OPPORTUNITY.

By 1984, the domestic expansion of my business was taking new directions. We had more than one hundred permanent centers and about six hundred part-time satellite locations serving ninety-five thousand students a year. In the last forty-five years, more than one million students had been tutored by Kaplan for an endless array of tests.

I had my eyes on even bigger opportunities in new markets and products. I felt there was a demand for my services in uncharted geographic and academic areas. I wanted to open centers internationally and upgrade my existing centers with computers. I also wanted to diversify my services beyond test preparation. But this would cost money, lots of money. I began to ask myself: How much investment was I willing and able to make?

I began looking at the numbers. Kaplan's annual revenues were $35 million, I owned the large building on West Fifty-sixth Street in Manhattan, and I was receiving annual air rights payments. But I rented most of my centers and classrooms under long-term leases—and they occupied hundreds of thousands of square feet of space. If the demand for test preparation took a downturn and Kaplan had several bad years of business, I would still be obligated to pay millions of dollars in rent and other costs. My audiotapes, while still an effective teaching tool, were no longer cutting edge. Computers were the wave of the future for communication, accounting, and teaching. My staff and I undertook extensive studies to evaluate the best computer programs and equipment. We quickly realized it would take a lot more get up-and-go than we had horses to ride. The competition was bearing down harder than I had ever imagined, with their inflated score claims, diversified services, and franchises across the nation, often right near our locations.

The teaching style that was synonymous with Kaplan and our personal service were two of our greatest assets. But for Kaplan to continue to grow, it would need a major infusion of capital and technical expertise. I'd never envisioned that my tutoring business would grow as large as it did. For years I'd never even considered myself a major entrepreneur. Now I was not sure I had the expertise to carry the business into new arenas. Kaplan had thousands of workers who depended on the security of a thriving, solvent company. I felt an awesome, overwhelming commitment to my staff, my students, my family, the company, and myself.

Periodically, someone would approach me about buying the company, but I always turned them down because I wasn't ready to let it go. Kaplan was my baby. It was my life and the lives of many others. But not selling could also have a devastating effect on my employees. A persistent voice nagged at me, reminding me that eventually I would need to consider passing the torch to a parent company that could aggressively propel Kaplan to new heights and ensure a safe future for my employees and my family.

Opportunity came knocking when I least expected it. Soon after the celebration of my sixty-fifth birthday in May 1984, I received a call from the Washington Post Company, which was owned and operated—and still is—by the renowned Graham family. Katharine Graham had inherited this $2 billion company, which published the world-famous *Washington Post* newspaper.

The offer to buy Kaplan was the brainchild of Richard D. Simmons, the company's president and chief operating officer, who identified Kaplan as a bright prospect to add to the company's portfolio. Kaplan was the kind of company that appealed to Simmons because he was moving the Washington Post Company to a new phase of growth and higher earnings. In 1967, the Washington Post Company had bought *Newsweek* magazine for $65 million, and it had prospered under Washington Post Company control. But beginning in 1980, under the steady hand of Simmons, the Washington Post Company had launched an even more aggressive market approach. Simmons was selling off faltering enterprises and buying subsidiaries in the fields of cellular telephones, computer communications, database publishing, and cable television. Simmons envisioned Kaplan as an important addition to that assemblage because it would be the Washington Post Company's first foray into education. He looked at our finances and operational structure and liked what he saw. Kaplan had a steady revenue growth, and the organizational structure was ripe for expansion. With the national education system at risk, its infrastructure needed an infusion of billions of dollars from private and public institutions. Education was becoming a very sexy word in the private business sector, and Kaplan was the leader in the for-profit category.

Simmons acted with speed and conviction. Katharine Graham later wrote in her autobiography that she hadn't really been interested in Kaplan, but if Simmons thought it would be profitable, she felt they should buy it. She later admitted that the company had much more substance and viability than she had initially realized. Not only was it a moneymaker, but it was setting high standards in the world of for-profit education.

The Washington Post Company was not our first suitor. There had been other, smaller companies interested in buying, but the Washington Post Company was different. With this company I sensed a feeling of trust. Other suitors didn't seem to have the dedication to preserve the integrity of Kaplan or to allow for a smooth and painless acquisition of a family-owned business. I felt that Simmons understood my desire to maintain my company's traditional high standards and to retain employees who had worked with me for years to build the business. I also liked the idea of selling Kaplan to a company in the communications business. I wanted a company with more than just money and expertise. I wanted a company that understood the value of educating and communication. That's what Kaplan was all about.

I also sensed that Simmons had vision. He understood the potential and future of for-profit education. He saw tremendous growth potential in foreign markets, especially Japan, Western Europe, and the Middle East. For each foreign student who came to the United States to study, perhaps sixteen would enroll in centers in their own countries. This expansion into foreign markets could be facilitated by the brain trust of *Newsweek International* and *The Washington Post*—two entities far more recognizable on the international scene than Kaplan. Simmons also planned to grab more of the SAT preparation market, develop our advertising, and use new technology as a teaching tool.

Negotiations continued for six months. We met in a local bistro near my office a number of times and talked about the nitty-gritty details. We finally ended our discussions with a firm handshake. Although there was some tough give-and-take in the negotiations, things ran smoothly because we both wanted the deal to happen. On November 20, 1984, we publicly announced an agreement in principle.

The agreement gave me additional resources, technological and marketing expertise, and continued independence for ten years. Kaplan became a subsidiary but functioned as a separate unit. My key employees retained their executive-level positions, and I remained president and chief executive officer. I had surrounded myself with loyal family and staff who had been a tremendous asset during more than forty years of unbelievable growth, and I didn't want that to change. The Washington Post Company put some of its staff into key positions, but I continued to direct our programs.

We also agreed not to advertise Kaplan as a "Washington Post" company because I thought it sounded too commercial, and I didn't want to take on a new image as a big, profit-making company. I realized later that that was a mistake on my part. Advertising Kaplan as a Washington Post company could have been an excellent marketing approach, and today most Kaplan ads and brochures include that designation. The Washington Post Company was and still is a quality company with an enviable worldwide reputation. In the test preparation field, Kaplan was the biggest and best. Being acquired by the Washington Post Company just added more credibility and prestige to the Kaplan name, which was by now so generic that other companies looked like copycats.

The sale prompted surprised looks both inside and outside the Washington Post Company. But the union of the Washington Post Company and Stanley H. Kaplan Educational Centers was a merger dedicated to quality that I believed would ensure Kaplan's tradition of excellence and growth.

Once the sale was completed in December 1984, Rita and I were invited to a welcoming party at the *Washington Post* headquarters in downtown Washington, D.C. About three hundred people attended, including journalistic luminaries such as Bob Woodward, one of the reporters who broke the Watergate stories, and political columnist David Broder. Of course, Katharine Graham attended with Richard Simmons and her son, Donald. The Washington Post Company employees gathered in the lobby in a getting-to-know-you session. Many had children who had taken my courses.

We were in the presence of so many people who had made their mark. From our conversation, our hosts and their staff seemed to feel the same way about us.

I walked into my office with mixed feelings the first business day after the merger. I was still president and CEO but no longer "the boss." I didn't own the chair I was sitting in, and I would no longer be the one to make final decisions as I had done in the past. It was a difficult transition psychologically but one I would have to accept. Even though I thought the Washington Post Company would be making good choices, it would be difficult to be left out of the major decisions.

I received a call from Marty Cohen, chief financial officer of the Washington Post Company, and we exchanged thoughts about what would make the new Kaplan organization work more smoothly. Marty was the catalyst behind Kaplan meeting budget projections. Until now, I had never given thought to budgets and profits and losses. My best business sense had always come from the gut. I'd just done what I thought was right, and it usually was right. Although I had possessed an entrepreneurial spirit since childhood, my true love was teaching, and I had relied heavily on my staff to run the business. Without them Kaplan would never have thrived. Now I was ushered into a bigger, more serious world of business! That was scary, and luckily I had some of my best and closest associates—Barry Wexler, Fred Danzig, Deborah Bond-Upson, Ruth Drucker, Carol Weinbaum—and my family to help me. It was particularly comforting to have Marty for meaningful support and advice in some difficult times.

My son, Paul, decided not to remain full-time with the company soon after I sold it to the Washington Post Company. He resigned in 1986 as controller but remained as a company consultant. He had worked with the company for eleven years and had been a tremendous asset to Kaplan. But his true love was the theater and the arts. During his undergraduate studies at the University of Pennsylvania, he had been a movie and theater critic for the *Daily Pennsylvanian* and, as a teenager, would quote from memory every detail from *Variety*. From his first day at Kaplan he had supplemented his sixty-hour workweek with duties in the theater. Now he wanted to apply his artistic talents to theatrical and motion picture production. His avocation became his vocation, and although I hated to see him leave Kaplan, I was happy to see him follow his heart.

The Washington Post Company stuck to every letter of our contract and so did Kaplan, which accounted for its continued growth. The Washington Post Company brought needed changes to outdated operations at Kaplan. Our accounting procedures hadn't been changed in years, and we had no computerized systems. Everything was done by hand in the most laborious manner. For example, each center and its satellite branches had two checking accounts, one controlled by the main office and the other controlled by the center administrator. Under this system, a single vendor could receive as many as nine separate checks—some for as little as $2—when Kaplan paid its bills.

I became the company cheerleader. I toured the nation attending conventions, giving interviews, making speeches, and visiting Kaplan centers. I wanted Kaplan to be the household word for test preparation. "Have attaché case, will travel" was my motto. New York City became a speck on my horizon. I journeyed from city to city, riding the media waves and getting a little seasick along the way even though I loved the excitement. One week I visited five cities in the South and Midwest. First I went to our Fort Lauderdale center to review plans to dot the Atlantic shoreline with satellite branches from Hollywood to Palm Beach. I left for Memphis at 4 A.M. the next day and stopped at Minneapolis, Detroit, and Toledo. In each city there was a media event, with interviews on television and radio talk shows. I took along some tricks that our new public relations firm in New York had taught me about how to get our message across. Even if a reporter's question was about the weather, I would mention our average point increases and remind listeners that we don't beat the SAT, we master it. When asked about our centers, I had a prepared thirty-second sound bite: "We prepare students for tests, instill confidence, prevent anxieties, improve knowledge, and work on test-taking strategies." If I talked fast enough, it clocked in at fifteen seconds. Some appearances were longer than fifteen seconds. When I appeared on a talk show in Kansas City, I informed, argued, and joked for four hours straight, until well after midnight, answering calls from listeners. One caller said he had dated my wife—before she married me, of course. Some listeners called our centers the next day to enroll in our classes.

I was Kaplan's biggest promoter, assuming roles as troubleshooter, road warrior, lightning rod, and diplomat. I was really popular on the media circuit when a new book on standardized testing was released that slammed the venerable ETS and stirred up more debates about coaching and the reliance on SAT scores.

I appeared on a CNN program with ETS president Gregory Anrig, who made candid and positive statements about coaching. Although he didn't wholeheartedly endorse my program, I thought it took a lot of courage for him to say what he did.

"Mr. Kaplan has been quite responsible in his claims that he has made over the years," Anrig said. "He says he is in the education business, not the coaching business. I think what Mr. Kaplan does is educationally sound, and I have no problem with that."

The College Board had already conceded that coaching could have a positive effect. But to hear Anrig say this about me on national television was a sweet victory. It may have appeared that I was a little too cozy with the ETS, but a good public image was important to set Kaplan apart from the disreputable practices of other test preparation companies.

In 1985, the ETS sued The Princeton Review and a smaller company called Pre-Test Review for copyright violations after the companies allegedly used questions from ETS exams without permission. The ETS alleged that an executive of one company himself took the SAT a number of times. The companies' officials said they had been unfairly targeted by the ETS because their coaching was effective.

I was pleased to see that the ETS finally took action because several years before I had gone to the ETS twice to complain about companies stealing test questions. My first visit to ETS was congenial. I asked it to police its tests better because my competitors were making a mockery of the whole preparation industry. When a company's success hinged on the reputation that students who took their courses could get the answers to the tests, that tainted the whole industry. ETS officials said they appreciated my concerns, but in the end they did nothing more than slap the violators on the wrist. The ETS kept the affairs under wraps because it feared copycat actions.

In 1985, I made a return visit to the ETS to register louder complaints about competitors' stealing questions. "They're stealing your questions right and left," I said. "Why don't you do something about them? Are you afraid of them?" ETS officials were more responsive this time, saying they realized the severity of the problem and telling me they had just filed a law-suit against The Princeton Review. It hurt the ETS's business as much as mine if students had prior knowledge of test questions.

This time there were consequences. Pre-Test Review settled with the ETS, and in a consent order, The Princeton Review agreed to pay the ETS $52,000 and was barred from using the test questions. The damages were minimal, but I used the opportunity to issue a statement urging parents and students to recognize the benefits and value of coaching in spite of these isolated incidents of unfair conduct. When news reporters asked me how the Kaplan approach differed from our competitors', I explained that our materials were not lifted from tests but painstakingly developed by a staff of researchers. I was never a big promoter of the ETS, but I applauded it when it did the right thing, and this time it did the right thing.

$$\bigcirc\bigcirc\bigcirc\bigcirc$$

In December 1985, my mother died peacefully at the age of ninety-two. It was difficult for me to distill all the memories of a person who had had a powerful influence on my life. Myriad flashbacks reminded me that this ninety-pound, four-foot, eight-inch woman had lived a life of courage, cheerfulness, and feisty independence. I could still feel her spoken and un-spoken words of approval of a job well done, and I missed her acknowledgments.

Her humor never failed her. What words can describe a woman who told the doctor who ordered a liver scan, "Why don't you liver me alone?" At her ninetieth birthday party, a friend said he hoped to attend her hundredth birthday celebration, and she shot back, "If you take good care of yourself, you will." Her spirit was an integral part of my being, and her legacy lives on in the many people she touched. We are all richer for that.

KAPLAN SHINES

I was the new kid entering the corporate classroom. For the first time, I was surrounded by unfamiliar faces and names, and I had to take orders and learn at someone else's pace. I was learning to work with people both inside and outside the company as I set my sights on new goals.

As I traveled the country promoting the Kaplan programs, I was amazed at the number of educators who had never heard of Kaplan Educational Centers. One of my ambitions was to make sure that every secondary school knew about Kaplan PSAT, SAT, and ACT courses and that most of our classes were only a bicycle ride away. Almost a third of the students taking the LSAT enrolled in our courses. I wanted a big proportion like that for undergraduate admissions test preparation as well.

I had other goals too. I wanted Kaplan to continue to garner the respect of the academic community. I wanted Kaplan to be accessible to most of the high school population. And I wanted Kaplan to expand in spite of, and because of, the growing competition.

First I advised my center administrators throughout the nation to call on student counselors and advisers, attend their regional meetings, and introduce them to Kaplan. "You can't be pushy," I wrote in my in-house newsletter, entitled *SHK News and Dos*. "Usually there's no problem if the adviser appreciates the assistance we try to give students, although several years ago I recall meeting some advisers, who studiously avoided us. Now we are very well received, and many seek us out to swap observations." Kaplan continued to show advisers that although test preparation books and tapes were in abundant supply, there was a distinct advantage to the structure, discipline, group reinforcement, and teacher guidance provided through test prep classes.

Kaplan representatives were also attending College Board conferences. It was a clear indication of how far we had come. The organization still did not officially endorse commercial coaching schools, but it published a host of preparation guides that competed with Kaplan. The moderator at one College Board meeting said that everyone should have preparation either in school or by private instructors. This statement would have come as a shock-a-roo years before. But now, as one educator put it, "We've lost our virginity when it comes to test preparation."

Standardized tests had become more influential than ever. In 1985, 13 percent more colleges used the SAT in admissions decisions than five years before. About half a billion standardized tests were being given each year to determine everything from job placement to school district funding and teachers' salaries. More than half of the standardized tests were mandated by state or local authorities to measure achievement, competency, and basic skills. Fifteen states required students to pass standardized tests for high school graduation.

By the mid-1980s, America's system of public higher education was more democratic than ever. College enrollment was at an all-time high, with minority enrollment at almost 18 percent. But there were still chasms. I couldn't reverse all of society's shortcomings, but I could expand the Kaplan programs dedicated to helping underrepresented students. We provided several million dollars' worth of tuition aid each year.

Kaplan was commissioned by the Southern Foundation to provide a reduced-tuition SAT preparation program for seventy-five disadvantaged students from Appalachia. We pulled out all the stops, sending eight experienced teachers to work with the students six hours a day. The instruction was intensive, but that's what was needed. One student who was legally blind insisted on being given no special attention and improved by 150 points. The students learned the most important lesson of all: you get out of the course what you put into it. We also teamed up with organizations such as the Urban League, the Cherokee Nation, and American Literacy Volunteers to help students prepare for tests.

Rita and I used the proceeds from the sale of our company to establish the Rita J. and Stanley H. Kaplan Family Foundation to support programs in education, health, the arts, and Jewish causes. It was a natural extension of the community causes we had been involved in for years. For example, I joined the board of the Brooklyn Philharmonic Orchestra in 1965 and was president and then chairman for twenty years. We donated an acoustical shell that elevated the Brooklyn Academy of Music concert hall to one of the finest music facilities in the city.

Establishing the foundation allowed us to contribute more time and money to causes we supported. The foundation's first venture was the creation of the Rita and Stanley H. Kaplan Cancer Center at the New York University Medical Center. It was the brainchild of Martha Selig, a friend and philanthropic mentor, who was the linchpin of many causes we espoused. My mother and many of my friends had been treated for cancer at New York University Medical Center, and I wanted to help in the advancement of research and cancer treatment. Our work is but a drop in the bucket, but the center is a leader in the fight against cancer and is known worldwide.

It was appropriate that the Kaplan foundation also be a leader in educational advancement. I became active in fund-raising for City College, raising money for scholarships and research. The foundation also supports programs of the Teachers College of Columbia University that provide academic training for economically disadvantaged students. More than half of the students who participate in the Albert G. Oliver (AGO) Program are the first in their families to attend college. Every year, about one-third of the Oliver Scholars attend selective secondary schools and are leaders at their schools—editor of the newspaper, class president, captain of the basketball team. Their college acceptances read like Oscar-winning admissions to colleges like Harvard, Yale, and Stanford.

The Kaplan Foundation is an active supporter of venerable art institutions in New York, and established the Stanley H. Kaplan Penthouse atop the Rose Building at Lincoln Center in Manhattan as a community meeting space. At the penthouse dedication, the opera star Luciano Pavarotti presented the Kaplan Foundation with one of his paintings, and I was surprised to discover that the tenor paints about as well as he sings. Sometimes the penthouse is so booked with events that Rita and I have to wait six months to schedule fund-raisers for the causes we want to promote. That's particularly ironic when people mistake the penthouse for our private residence. A friend called me to say he had heard that the presidents of the United States and China held a meeting at the Stanley H. Kaplan Penthouse. He wondered why I hadn't told him about my distinguished houseguests. We both laughed when I explained that the penthouse was not my home and that I had learned about the presidents' visit only when I read about it in the newspaper.

At least half of the Kaplan Foundation's grants are allocated to Jewish causes, including programs in Israel and the United States for women's education, child care, civil rights, and Jewish education. The Foundation supports the Solomon Schecter School in New York and Rashi School in Boston, nonsecular Jewish day schools that have been highly successful in keeping the Jewish traditions alive. We also support the Sutton Place Synagogue, which is constructing a multimillion-dollar religious school. I am a member of the advisory board of Ben Gurion University of the Negev, which has received worldwide recognition for its projects in desalinization of water, dry desert farming, and the harvesting of solar energy in Third World countries. Rita's involvement with Jewish social services for more than forty years has made possible the construction of a Brooklyn Center for Social Services only six blocks from where I started my first Kaplan center.

○○○○

Even though the mid-1980s was a period of economic slowdown, Kaplan's earning performance delighted the Washington Post Company. Our gains headed skyward in 1987 and 1988 as we enrolled 100,000 students a year. Kaplan was a $45 million enterprise with five hundred locations. We had helped more than 1.5 million students achieve their aspirations. Among those students were the children of former New York Governor Mario Cuomo, whom I met at a social function and who said as he shook my hand, "It's good to meet the man who has all my money."

Under the sale agreement, payments were to be delivered in two parts— one at the time of the sale and a second payment three years later if revenues matched projections. We met this goal by raising tuition, which had hardly changed in several years while enrollment had kept increasing. For years I had kept prices low, fearing a market reaction in the shadow of increased competition. But the prices I charged had not kept pace with inflation or the new, higher costs of adding computers and expanding services.

I attended a Washington Post Company managers' meeting twice a year and was gratified to see a glowing headline on a slide presentation: "Kaplan Shines." My vest buttons popped and I wore a big smile. I was delivering what our division had targeted: needed services and a handsome bottom line. I enjoyed mixing with the heads of other major divisions and with Katharine Graham and her son Donald. One of the most amazing men I ever met was Warren Buffett, a principal stockholder of the Washington Post Company. I remember him dazzling us with a plan to make the U.S. government a publicly held company.

The Washington Post Company worked with our staff to make changes and additions. Kaplan tapped into the new world of cyberspace by creating an Internet site—commonplace now but a rarity when the term "Web site" meant nothing more than a spider's home.

LSAT preparation accounted for almost a third of our enrollment, and we increased our enrollment for national medical board preparation. We added new courses, including CPA test preparation. In 1989, we established Kaplan International to serve foreign students in America. Our visions of taking Kaplan abroad became a reality. We opened international centers in Panama and Korea to help students prepare for American tests in their own countries. We entered licensing agreements with educational training companies to offer prep courses overseas for the GRE, GMAT, CGFNS (Commission on Graduates of Foreign Nursing Schools Qualifying Exam), and TOEFL (Test of English as a Foreign Language). This international expansion marked the beginning of licensee relationships with leading educational institutions in Europe, South America, Asia, and the Middle East.

Of course, our successes prompted fiercer competition. Because I was *the* Stanley H. Kaplan behind the Kaplan company name, my competitors targeted me in their advertisements. "Stanley's Finally Lost It," one ad blurted. "Stanley Kaplan's a Wimp," bellowed another. I tried not to take it personally and remembered William Shakespeare's quote—they were "full of sound and fury, signifying nothing."

During a Washington Post Company board meeting, I expressed my concerns about the aggressive nature of our competitors. But the consensus among the Post executives was that bad guys finish last and that Kaplan had always taken the high road. We didn't want to wallow in a mud fight with companies that might shoot themselves in the foot if left alone. But we decided to go nose to nose with competitors by promoting our superior preparation programs and services with our own ads.

We assembled a first-rate public relations and marketing team bolstered by an outside advertising agency. We wanted Kaplan, Kaplan, Kaplan to be seen at every turn. Our new T-shirts reiterated our television and radio advertisements: "If You Care—Prepare." Buses were plastered with ads declaring, "Take Kaplan and Get a Higher Score." Billboards and posters appeared in nontraditional venues such as the New York City subway and a giant billboard on the New Jersey Turnpike. A clever, eye-catching July Fourth advertisement in the *New York Times* read, "Congratulations to the Lady of Liberty from the Father of Test Prep."

The Washington Post Company made another important decision in 1991 that wouldn't reveal its full significance for another three years. Alan G. Spoon, then president and chief operating officer, asked Jonathan Grayer, a twenty-six-year-old employee at Newsweek Inc., to join Kaplan as regional operations director. Grayer was a Harvard Business School graduate who had been with *Newsweek* only a year and a half, but Spoon was impressed with his creativity when it came to cutting costs. Once Grayer joined Kaplan, he quickly rose in the ranks to become vice president of marketing.

I wasn't aware of Spoon's decision at the time. I was preoccupied with my son, Paul, who had been diagnosed with the HIV virus, which causes AIDS. I spent months at Paul's hospital bedside, grappling with the inexplicable illness of my son, who was so young. He was only thirty-six years old when he died, and we all mourned the talent this world lost. He had been an associate producer of *As Is*, a drama at Broadway's Lyceum Theatre about the impact of AIDS. He had also been the executive producer of the 1986 movie *Parting Glances* and an executive committee member of the Lesbian and Gay Community Services Center. He was also instrumental in establishing the gay and lesbian synagogue in Manhattan.

Paul was the only tennis partner willing to play with a hack like me, and sometimes we rallied until the wee hours of the morning. We both shared a love of music, theater, and film. For years he had been my invaluable business associate. But more important, he was my only son, and there is nothing more tragic or unnatural than the premature death of a child or a grandchild. Fortunately, the Kaplan "family"—the wonderful people who had helped create the Kaplan enterprise—surrounded Rita and me in our period of mourning. Katharine Graham arrived at my home after the funeral to express her condolences. We talked about Paul and his contribution to the Kaplan organization and the world around him.

○○○○

Attitudes toward test preparation continued to evolve. In 1993, the College Board changed the "A" in SAT from "Aptitude" to "Assessment." What's in a name? In this case, a lot. It signified reconciliation after years of resistance by the College Board. In the early 1980s, I had suggested to ETS President Gregory Anrig that the name be changed, and he had been keen on the idea. He told me excitedly during a College Board convention in 1989, "ETS has approved the name change, but we still have to convince the College Board." Now, four years later, it was done. "The College Board trustees wished to correct the impression among some people that the SAT measures something that is innate and impervious to change regardless of effort or instruction," the College Board president said in announcing the name change. The name change acknowledged that the SAT measured acquired knowledge and that it was not impervious to coaching. The College Board said the name change also illustrated new uses for the test to advise and assess students, place them in classes, and evaluate school curriculums.

The name change also inaugurated a new and improved SAT in 1994. The test was restructured into two parts requiring more critical reasoning than the old test. The SAT I: Reasoning Test tested both reading and math skills, and the SAT II: Subject Tests were achievement tests used for class placement. The two parts could be used separately or combined to assess a student's total academic skills. The SAT I was changed to emphasize reading skills that are so important in college-level studies. Some paired reading passages were added to test students' skill at making comparisons. Another new addition to the verbal skills section was testing students' knowledge of vocabulary words in the context of the reading passages. The math section of the new SAT I featured a Student-Produced Response section in which students wrote their answers in a grid box rather than selecting from a multiple-choice list of answers. Guessing was replaced by creating, because the student had to devise the answer. For the first time, students were permitted to use calculators during the test. I applauded the changes because the test more accurately measured the math and verbal skills needed for college work.

A new test, a new name, and we were poised for a new Kaplan.

13

CHANGING OF THE GUARD

A decade had passed since I had sold my business to the Washington Post Company. I had agreed to stay ten years, and the time was up. I was celebrating the thirty-fifth anniversary of my fortieth birthday, and it was time for a changing of the guard. After more than fifty-five years at the helm, I knew that Kaplan should use the talents of younger men and women who were eager to make their marks at Kaplan. I wanted to stay at Kaplan forever, but it was time for others to take over.

Accepting the reality of retirement was difficult. To me, retiring meant re-tiring, or putting on new tires. And I don't mean retreads. I couldn't possibly retire in the traditional sense. Because most of my life had been consumed with test preparation, I was eager to be part of the wider world. My time had to be productive. I have boundless energy, and I realized that there were all kinds of busyness to keep me active and mentally alert. I retained the title of chairman of the board of Kaplan and spent my time fulfilling the philanthropic goals of the Rita J. and Stanley H. Kaplan Family Foundation.

In the summer of 1994, Jonathan Grayer was named president and chief executive officer of Kaplan. He was preceded by two other presidents of Kaplan who had come on board to help me. Michaelita Quinn had been appointed in the late 1980s, and Gregory Rorke, the former president of Danskin hosiery company, had been appointed in the summer of 1992.

Alan Spoon said that his only initial hesitation about naming Grayer had been that he was only twenty-nine years old, but he quickly added that this would not be a major obstacle. Grayer was competent beyond his years and could make Kaplan leaner and more efficient. Grayer himself harbored no reservations about his new assignment. He was smart, self-assured, and articulate and had earned his spurs at *Newsweek* and Kaplan. He possessed as much confidence in the company as in himself. He saw growth opportunities that had barely been touched. We had spoken about the competition, and I felt that he would be quick to respond if challenged or provoked. He had the blessing of the Washington Post Company, which would give him the financial backing to carry the company forward. I could feel the future coming fast.

Grayer's first move was to bring in a group of determined Harvard MBAs from American Express, Goldman Sachs, Morgan Stanley, and RJR Nabisco. A few people who had been with Kaplan since the 1960s rose to new executive positions, but my family members followed other interests outside the company.

Big changes came within the first few months. Kaplan turned its attention to in-house matters and completely reorganized operations. One move was to eliminate the independent contractor status of center administrators and absorb the staff as Kaplan employees, raising the payroll from five hundred to nearly three thousand people, which better reflected the true size of Kaplan. This enabled the company to function like a spoke-and-wheel design, with Kaplan having central control over all the centers. Before the change, Kaplan had had ninety independent contractors whose commissions over the years had been reduced to 13 percent of the gross revenues to offset rising costs. The center administrators' earnings had been good, but the company's profits had been diminishing. The new design allowed Kaplan to outfit each center with state-of-the-art computers and streamline accounting and marketing systems.

Grayer put all that Ivy League talent to work. His first task was to shore up the mantle of Kaplan —test preparation. We were still the biggest players in the test preparation game, with $90 million in annual revenues despite lackluster gains in recent years. But we were facing the greatest challenges from competitors in our SAT business, and we wanted to reclaim the major stake.

Test preparation was no longer confined to the classroom. The competition had already made forays into sales of books, tapes, and computer software so students could prepare for tests without taking more costly courses. Competitors distributed an array of preparation books and computer software, and Kaplan needed to play catch-up. We launched Kaplan

Inter-Active to produce computer software, books, and on-line communications.

Kaplan wasn't content to sit back and watch The Princeton Review run amok. Grayer was committed to stepping up our response to attacks from competitors. We wanted to quash the relentless and misleading advertisements. "The Princeton Review has spent years getting in our face by running rude ads about Stanley Kaplan," Grayer told reporters. "They've run ads that made my blood boil. Now the battle is engaged. We're mad as hell and we're not going to take it anymore. Our company invented the industry and we're back to claim what's rightfully ours. We've decided we will no longer allow The Princeton Review to run wild in the industry."

Kaplan threatened to sue The Princeton Review if it didn't pull its ads featuring unsubstantiated score improvement claims and agree to prove future score increase claims with adequately supported studies. Wanting to avoid a messy legal battle, both sides agreed that further disputes would be settled through legal arbitration. That was cheaper than court battles, but it would still cost both companies more than a half-million dollars in legal fees to hash out the differences.

An arbitration panel ruled that The Princeton Review could no longer advertise inflated score improvements. It was an important victory for Kaplan as well as for students, who deserved fair and honest advertising. The panel also found that our Price Waterhouse study on score improvements was sound. The landmark ruling leveled the playing field and set reputable standards in the test preparation industry.

One of Kaplan's goals was to continue to ensure test quality. Over the years, our staff of researchers had pointed out flaws in the tests to the test makers, who were continuously revising tests and grade formulas to make them more reliable. When Kaplan discovered that questions in a new practical judgment section of the GMAT inadvertently gave clues to the answers, we notified the test makers so they could rewrite the questions. The test makers didn't like our scrutiny of their products, but our watchful eyes helped make better, fairer tests for test takers. On another occasion, one of our researchers discovered that questions in the logic section of the GRE could be easily answered using systematic tricks. A longtime Kaplan executive, Fred Danzig, called an ETS official and told him about the flaw.

"Come on over and show us what you found," the ETS official said. Fred showed the ETS the problem and said, "Is this going on the new test coming out on Monday?"

"We were planning on that," the ETS official said.

"Well, I wouldn't do that if I were you," Fred said. The ETS saw the flaw, heeded our advice, and pulled the item from the test.

Kaplan was also mindful of test quality during the 1994 introduction of computerized testing. The GRE was the first ETS test that students took on a computer. The computer-adaptive test does just what the name says. It adapts to the students' abilities as they take the test. The test questions get progressively harder as a student answers questions correctly and should get easier when a student answers questions incorrectly. This format was designed to test a wider range of skills with fewer questions, and it assured more accurate scoring. But that meant that students could not jump back to double-check their answers or skip over questions they couldn't answer. We eventually installed banks of computers in our centers to teach students how to take these new computer-adaptive tests.

Kaplan saw the benefits of computer-adaptive testing but wanted it done right. Kaplan employees took the test and discovered that the database of questions was so small that some questions were recycled from previous tests. Even students who did not intend to cheat could inadvertently share test questions. We didn't pass this information on to our students. Instead, the staff re-created portions of the test that it believed were faulty and delivered these examples to the ETS to demonstrate the test's vulnerabilities.

At first the ETS welcomed the information and thanked us for our study. But when news of the test's problems hit the media, the ETS filed a multimillion-dollar lawsuit against Kaplan in U.S. District Court charging copyright infringement and violation of electronic-communication privacy laws. We hadn't printed or distributed the questions, merely returned re-created questions to the test makers to demonstrate the depth of problems. The ETS was accusing us of violating copyright laws when all we had done was show ETS a version of their own test.

Eventually, the case was settled out of court. And although the ETS refused to admit the test had been compromised by its own oversights, it administered the GRE on a reduced schedule. It also delayed by years its plans to convert the GRE to an exclusively computer-based test. In keeping with the Kaplan tradition, we once again were leaders in protecting rights for test takers, in assuring quality tests, and in legitimizing the role of the test prep industry.

Grayer's aggressive, high-profile entrance at Kaplan paid off. Revenues rose by 8 percent in 1994 and 11 percent in 1995, to $90 million, and profits were in the mid-seven figures. Kaplan's growth reflected the company's tradition of breaking new ground as a national leader in test preparation.

Meanwhile, Rita and I were busy breaking new ground with our foundation. We expanded our offices to a five-room suite in a building adjacent to our home in Manhattan. The rooms of the office are lined with photos of our travels, family, and friends and mementos of the company. The foundation allows me to continue the most interesting aspect of my life and work, which is helping people.

One afternoon in the early 1990s a young student from Princeton University named Wendy Kopp arrived at my office to ask me to sponsor an advertisement for a conference on business's role in education reform. I agreed, and later Wendy returned with a bigger request. She had written a class thesis in which she proposed forming a national teaching corps with some of the country's brightest college graduates teaching for two years in underresourced urban and rural schools. It would be like an education Peace Corps. She was determined to make it a reality. She had already received some corporate grant money, but she needed more. Wendy was so enthusiastic and convincing that I couldn't refuse to help provide seed money. But I wanted to contribute more than just dollars. Like me, Wendy was breaking new ground in education, and I wanted to help her from the basement up. I sponsored "retreats" at a hotel in Washington, D.C., as brainstorming sessions with students from the best universities who might be interested in teaching upon graduation. Although some of them aspired to be doctors, lawyers, and businessmen, they were interested in the idea because they were committed to helping schools in need and they could receive education awards to pay or defer student loans in exchange for teaching. She formed Teach for America, a nonprofit organization that today has placed more than six thousand college graduates in urban and rural public schools across the nation. She has raised $76 million from foundations, cor-porations, government grants, and individuals.

I was amazed how often Rita and I were guided in our foundation work by some unexplainable set of coincidences. When our congregation built a house of worship commemorating Paul near our Pennsylvania country home, Paul's closest friend and fellow student at James Madison High School arrived at the dedication ceremony without knowing the synagogue was dedicated to Paul. Heavy rains threatened the transfer of Torahs from the old synagogue to the new. Inexplicably, just as the ceremony was sched-uled to begin, the clouds parted, a narrow patch of blue appeared, and sun-shine streamed down on our shoulders. The Torahs could now be moved from the old synagogue to the new. Immediately after the transfer, the sky darkened and rain came. Those were two remarkable strokes of divine in-tervention in one day. Sometimes things happen that you believe never could. I'm a skeptic at heart, but somehow I feel that mysterious forces can direct our lives and our destiny.

So I was busy, busy, busy with the foundation and keeping up with Kaplan's latest changes. But not too busy to share thoughts with a good friend over lunch or take in a good movie. And on long weekends there was tennis, golf, gardening, and photography. Or making a trip to Boston to visit my daughters and their families. My children and grandchildren walk too fast and play tennis too well. But Rita and I can talk as fast as any of them. Get Rita into a conversation, she's a terror! My advice to young people is to make sure their families are close-knit. Work is important, but take time to be together as a family. That's not easy because we all want to be successful in a profession or business. One must make a special effort to establish strong family ties and a deep conviction in beliefs and faith.

Because my family worked by my side, I saw them a lot. But the time was not always "family time," and I wish I had created more pleasure time with them. It was difficult to strike the perfect balance between work and family when a growing business created so many demands. Sometimes the business consumed all our time. But overall we were lucky to enjoy the re-wards of family and hard work.

Kaplan was enjoying the rewards of hard work too. By 1996, the com-pany had 185 test preparation centers and 1,000 classroom sites throughout the world. But why stop there? For-profit education meant a diversified, multilayered education organization that served more than just anxious parents and students preparing for tests.

There were three ways to build this broader-based entity: deliver education to the masses, utilize the latest technology, and diversify our services and customer base. Kaplan wanted meritocracy in education without mediocrity. Nontraditional customers were just waiting for us to come knocking. Kaplan wanted to help the fourth-grader struggling with math, the waiter who aspired to become an attorney, the foreign doctor who wanted to practice in America, and the single mother who wanted to return to college in the evening. America's baby boomers were now parents with an obsession for success for themselves and their children through education and career advancement. It helped that they had the prosperity and incredible energy to reach those goals. In many aspects, the parents of today are no different from the Brooklyn parents who brought their children to me in the 1940s and 1950s seeking better education for their children.

The Kaplan brand name allowed for a natural extension into the diversified services of college admissions assistance, career services, and basic skills instruction. In 1996, Kaplan entered a copublishing agreement with Simon & Schuster, then the world's largest educational and English-language book publisher, to publish books on careers, education, and life skills. By 1999, there were one hundred titles in print and ten software titles on topics such as test prep, college admissions, and career guidance. Among those publications were guides for taking the New York State Regents Exams. What a long road from the 1940s, when I began writing Regents guides, to Kaplan becoming one of the top four test preparation publication giants!

My first students had been play yard friends who needed help with their math homework. Kaplan continued that tradition of teaching basic skills in a fun atmosphere as it acquired SCORE! an after-school tutoring program for elementary and middle school students. The program caught on like wildfire and was so popular that we opened a new center every two weeks. By 1999, Kaplan had more than seventy SCORE! centers nationwide.

Kaplan was into education from every angle—outside the schools, inside the schools, and after school. So it was only natural that soon we *were* the school by using the latest technology. In 1998, we launched the nation's first online law school, Concord University School of Law. The tuition is substantially less than traditional law schools, and students "attend" Concord via the Internet to become eligible for a law degree in California. Concord reaches nontraditional students such as career professionals, family caregivers, and those who live or work too far away from a traditional law school. It was the first of its kind, and today it is the country's second largest part-time law school (based on the size of the first year entering class).

Kaplan continued to expand worldwide. Kaplan International formed a network of programs for foreign students studying in America and licensees opened more Kaplan centers all around the globe. A former Kaplan MCAT teacher in the Boston office saw the demand for test preparation outside the United States and in 1997 opened an 7,000-square-foot center in Bogotá, Colombia, fully equipped with twenty computers. He plans to open a center in Venezuela in 2001.

In other parts of the world, Kaplan centers sprang up as the Cold War ended. In 1998, a Kaplan licensee opened what its staff called "Kaplan Poland." Who would have thought of Kaplan in Poland? Students are now able to enroll in test preparation classes at Kaplan centers in eight Polish cities. All the centers have high-tech labs with computers, and one Nigerian student traveled from Vienna for Kaplan classes in Poland. The young couple who opened the Polish centers were trailblazers on the test prep frontier, as I had been years before.

I was glad to witness Kaplan's continued commitment to programs for disadvantaged students. In 1994, Kaplan adopted A. Philip Randolph Campus High School located on the City College campus in Harlem to provide free study skill seminars, mentoring, parent seminars, college scholarships, and donations of books and software. Today Kaplan has more than fifty national and local programs for thousands of economically disadvantaged and underrepresented minority students, and has provided more than $10 million in scholarships.

Just as I had used the latest technology to help teach students, Kaplan continued to incorporate the latest technology: computers and the Internet. On the first anniversary of Concord's founding, Kaplan launched on-line test preparation classes for six admissions exams. They cost less than half the price of our regular programs and provided students with twenty-four-hour access to multimedia lessons. Welcome to cyberspace! The same teaching techniques I developed years ago are used today, but now they are available to more people at a lower cost. Kaplan was becoming one of the largest distance education providers in the nation and was keeping pace with the anticipated 95 percent annual growth in the on-line education market. It launched KaplanCollege.edu, on-line educational programs for working professionals who want to advance their careers.

Kaplan had become such a large broad-based provider of education services and products—including several e-commerce businesses—that a name change was in order. The company originated as Stanley H. Kaplan Educational Center Ltd. because I wanted my full name and an emphasis on our role to educate. Then it shrank to Kaplan Educational Centers Inc. because our public relations department said, "It's not Henry Ford Corporation, it's Ford Corporation." I countered and said, "It's Estée Lauder, not Lauder; and Perry Ellis, not Ellis." Obviously, I lost the argument. And that's how our name then became Kaplan, Inc.

The Kaplan name is synonymous with education and was even used to make a point about learning during the historic 2000 presidential campaign. When the Republican candidate, George W. Bush, said he might have surprised observers with his sudden ability to converse about foreign policy, CBS News quoted a political science professor who said, "Obviously, he took the Stanley Kaplan course in foreign policy." Now, that's name recognition. One never knows where the Kaplan name will appear. In a cartoon by Jeff Shesol, a character named Thatch approaches a friend who is studying and asks, "You're taking Kaplan Review? Those courses cost a fortune!"

The friend responds, "I've got no choice, Thatch. If I'm ever gonna get into grad school, I've got to ace the entrance exam. Kaplan costs. But I've got to do everything in my power to be competitive. Everything!"

Thatch says, "You're not—"

"On steroids?" she interrupts. "No. They test for that stuff now."

The Kaplan name even provided good material on late-night television shows. My ears perked up when I heard David Letterman drop the Kaplan name in his list of funny back-to-school supplies, including the "Stanley Kaplan Guide to Filling Out Your McDonald's Application."

It is still exciting to see students' reactions when they meet Stanley H. Kaplan for the first time. Some are third-generation Kaplan students whose parents and grandparents I taught in Brooklyn. Many are surprised to learn I exist and that I am not some fictional test prep symbol. When I introduced myself to one young man at a charitable function, he took a few steps backward and said, "*The* Stanley Kaplan? I took your course in College Station, Texas, but I never knew you were real." It was quite an experience to meet someone whose life had been changed by Kaplan.

Another time I was riding on the subway carrying my signature Stanley H. Kaplan Educational Center tote bag when a young man asked me, "Are you taking a course?" I answered quite modestly, "Not quite." Then he asked me, "Have you met Stanley Kaplan?" I answered with a straight face, "Yes, every morning when I look in the mirror." I couldn't believe what happened next. This uninhibited young man shouted out to the other passengers, "Hey, we've got a famous person here. It's Stanley Kaplan!" I've learned to never underestimate the power of name recognition. Whenever a question about my identity arises, unless the person is over ninety years old or under five years old, chances are I answer, "Yup!" before he or she can even finish the question. Once I met a Stanley I. Kaplan who was not related, but we had something else in common: all four of his children had taken Kaplan courses.

Today the Kaplan name means so much more than test preparation. Kaplan is the country's premier provider of a variety of educational and career services for individuals, schools, and businesses that have served more than three million people. It's hard for me to comprehend that the small tutoring business I started in my basement more than sixty years ago now has five operating divisions with approximately ten thousand employees. Revenues for 2001 are projected to be more than $500 million. What is also amazing is that less than half of those revenues come from test preparation. Kaplan has diversified its for-profit education services into so many other areas of learning beyond test preparation. With twenty-seven acquisitions, Kaplan is now the second largest subsidiary of the Washington Post Company. And the Kaplan name is known outside America, with approximately thirty centers in nearly twenty countries. We continue to surpass even our largest competitors. In 1999, the total revenue for Kaplan's test prep unit exceeded $151 million, compared with The Princeton Review's revenues of $40 million. The operating income for Kaplan's test prep unit was $21 million, while The Princeton Review lost $2 million that year. The Washington Post Company executives were right: Bad guys do finish last.

And where in this new landscape of education and testing is the College Board? Our paths, once so divergent, have merged at the competitive cross-roads. The College Board—which for so long dismissed test preparation as ineffective—established a for-profit Internet subsidiary to promote its own test preparation services. To me, this was the ultimate validation of coaching. And the College Board instruction handbook, which is still distributed to students before they take the SAT, doesn't compare to its earlier publications that castigated coaching. Today the handbook states that while some students need only familiarize themselves with the test beforehand, others may benefit from systematic preparation. Some students can prepare on their own, it advises, while others need a structured approach. The handbook warns students to beware of claims of huge score increases but openly acknowledges that coaching can produce score increases. What a welcome statement to see in print after a hard-fought battle to change hearts and minds.

Part of that change came with America's increased reliance on standard-ized tests to judge our children's academic performance. Today, the debate over our dependence on standardized tests has reached a crescendo. The SAT has influenced the admissions process for decades and shows no signs of abatement. Today, almost four-fifths of the nation's 1,800 colleges and universities use the SAT for admissions purposes. And the prepon-derance of all kinds of standardized testing has trickled down to students of all ages. Three-year-olds are taking entrance exams for nursery school, and students in elementary and middle school are given standardized tests sometimes twice a year to rank students, schools, teachers, and adminis-trators. This discussion raises important questions, some mentioned by Ralph Nader, regarding the correlation between students' testing abilities and their promise for success. My grandson Scott Kaplan Belsky did not score 1600 on his SAT, but he blossomed into a remarkable leader and an ambitious entrepreneur. He often jokes that the pressure to perform well on the SAT was family-induced and not really related to college-application anxiety. He became president of his class at Cornell with a 3.7 GPA, was an alternate member of the Board of Trustees of the university, formed an investment club, and started a business called Living Big, manufacturing T-shirts.

But the increased use of test scores has caused a backlash. In the new millennium, more educators, parents, and students are questioning to what extent standardized tests, and specifically the SAT, should be used. In a dramatic and surprising departure, the president of California's public university system recommended that the SAT be eliminated in the admissions process and replaced by a test that mirrors the specific courses taken by high school students in California.

The College Board released a statement to reinforce its message that the SAT tests abstract reasoning and does not measure innate intelligence or other attributes critical to college success, such as creativity and motivation. I believe the SAT should continue to be used by college admissions officers with the caveat that the test has limitations and should be used in combination with other indicators of a student's performance and ability. The SAT is a vital yardstick when grade inflation is running rampant, and has been an effective tool to select students for years. Why abandon it now?

Witnessing the changes in test preparation and the tremendous growth of Kaplan was like attending my children's college graduations. As I sat in the audience proudly basking in their accomplishments, I was amazed at how quickly they had matured and prospered. As with my children, I reared the Kaplan enterprise from infancy, ushering it through childhood and pushing it into a larger world as a well-rounded adult with depth and character. Today, I watch in wonder and contentment as Kaplan continues to mature, knowing its future is bright.

I am proud of Kaplan's legacy of learning. I remember from my own childhood days how my self-confidence and self-esteem sprang from seizing knowledge and sharing it with others. But not everyone is as fortunate as I was to have parents and teachers nurturing me in the joy of learning. That's why I dedicated my life to helping students become their own best models of success. It really doesn't matter whether a student becomes a doctor or a carpenter as long as he or she lives up to his or her greatest potential. This philosophy was the guiding principle in both my personal and professional life.

Kaplan forged the paths in teaching reforms, test takers' rights, and test quality. But those were only the residual effects stemming from my driving desire to answer larger questions and solve bigger problems in education: How can we, as a culture, society, and community, teach kids to love learning? How do we help them believe in themselves enough to say, "Hey, I can tackle that"? How can we move forward with innovative approaches to teaching? Are we helping students to really understand what they are taught?

I created a consumer-oriented, for-profit education business that was not fettered by tradition or bureaucracy. I dedicated my life to meeting the needs of students in ways that traditional forms of education could not, and Kaplan continues in that tradition today. I hope that none of us will ever stop asking these pertinent questions—and discovering the appropriate answers—so that we can teach America's students in the most creative and effective ways possible.

I hope you will visit a Kaplan center soon!

Index

Trademarks Used in the Text

The American College Test (ACT) is a registered trademark of ACT, Inc.

The Allied Health Professions Admission Test (AHPAT) is a registered trademark of The Psychological Corporation.

The Commission on Graduates of Foreign Nursing Schools Qualifying Exam (CGFNS) is a registered trademark of the Educational Testing Service.

The Dental Admission Test (DAT) is a registered trademark of the American Dental Association.

The Graduate Management Admission Test (GMAT) is a registered trademark of the Graduate Management Admission Council.

The Graduate Record Examination (GRE) is a registered trademark of the Educational Testing Service.

The Law School Admission Test (LSAT) is a registered trademark of the Law School Admission Council.

The Medical College Admission Test (MCAT) is a registered trademark of the Association of American Medical Colleges.

The Miller Analogies Test (MAT) is a registered trademark of The Psychological Corporation.

New York State Regents Exams are administered by the University of the State of New York/State Education Department.

The Nursing Licensure Exam for Registered Nurses (NCLEX-RN) is a registered trademark of the National Council of the State Boards of Nursing (NCSBN.)

The PSAT/NMSQT is a trademark of the College Entrance Examination Board and National Merit Scholarship Corporation.

The SAT is a registered trademark of the College Entrance Examination Board.

The Test of English as a Foreign Language (TOEFL) is a registered trademark of the Educational Testing Service.

The United States Medical Licensing Examination (USMLE) is sponsored by the Federation of State Medical Boards (FSMB) of the United States, Inc., and the National Board of Medical Examiners® (NBME®).

About Anne Farris

Anne Farris is a freelance journalist whose work has appeared for more than two decades in newspapers, magazines, books, and international film documentaries. She has reported on state and national politics and government for a variety of newspapers, including the *New York Times,* the *Washington Post,* the *St. Louis Post-Dispatch,* and the *Arkansas Gazette,* and contributed to several books, including *Bloodsport,* published by Simon & Schuster in 1996. She has also reported for BBC documentaries and the 1998 English television documentary "The Clintons: A Marriage of Power." She lives in Chevy Chase, Maryland, with her two children.